how to hire a lawyer

W9-BEX-080

how to hire a lawyer

the consumer's guide to good counsel

by
Barry M. Gallagher

A DELTA/SEYMOUR LAWRENCE BOOK

A DELTA/SEYMOUR LAWRENCE BOOK
Published by
Dell Publishing Co., Inc.
1 Dag Hammarskjold Plaza
New York, New York 10017

Copyright © 1979 by Barry M. Gallagher

All rights reserved. No part of this book may be reproduced or transmitted in any form or by any means, electronic or mechanical, including photocopying, recording or by any information storage and retrieval system, without the written permission of the Publisher, except where permitted by law.

Delta ® TM 755118, Dell Publishing Co., Inc.

Printed in the United States of America

First Delta printing—October 1979

Library of Congress Cataloging in Publication Data

Gallagher, Barry M.
How to hire a lawyer.

Bibliography: page 224
Includes index
1. Attorney and client—United States.
I. Title.
KF311.G34   1979   347′.73′5   79-18631

ISBN 0-440-53774-6

To my mother and father

ACKNOWLEDGMENTS

My sincere gratitude to the many people who provided encouragement, assistance, advice, and friendship throughout the many months of manuscript preparation. In particular, I wish to thank Georgia Johnson, Isabella Cerruti, Michael Cronan, Eleanor Bailey, Pennfield Jensen, and Richard Barry.

And a special thanks to Melinda Self, Robin Loux, and Rochele Ullum for their tireless and proficient secretarial skills.

AUTHOR'S NOTE

Grammarians have not achieved a consensus on how to avoid the awkward "he/she" construction. Therefore, I have used the masculine pronoun throughout this book, purely for purposes of readability. Such usage should not be construed, nor is it intended, to minimize the role and increasing presence of America's woman lawyers.

Contents

Preface

The public's criticism of lawyers in particular, and the legal profession in general, is increasing at a rate which can only be construed as alarming by responsible members of the profession. This criticism centers on incompetence exhibited by some lawyers, excessive legal fees, failure to make needed legal services readily available to all, undue delay in resolving lawsuits, intolerable court congestion, and a failure to impose adequate discipline on lawyers engaged in misconduct.

As a practicing lawyer, it seems to me that much of this criticism is valid. Conversations with fellow lawyers confirm that they too are concerned over the failure of the profession, despite opportunity and ability, to respond effectively to this criticism by taking the action needed to remove its causes.

If the profession continues in its failure to deal decisively with valid criticism, its very status as a self-regulated group possessed of the near-exclusive right to practice law, and thereby provide the legal services needed by so many millions of Americans, will be challenged. Already there is evidence of such a challenge. Do-it-yourself books on legal topics, which explain how to perform tasks previously thought to be the exclusive domain of lawyers, are appearing in ever increasing numbers. Additionally, some state legislatures are beginning to enact laws streamlining the procedures for resolving legal disputes and other matters so that non-lawyers can perform services once thought to require a lawyer.

For many people, however, these self-help books and legislative efforts will not eliminate the need for a lawyer. When the need arises, they are simply at a loss to know how to find and hire the right lawyer. It was my realization that there existed no truly informative source explaining how to respond to the need for a lawyer, or to cope with problems arising in an existing lawyer/client relationship, which led me to write this book.

I believe the information contained here will enable you to deal effectively with a lawyer and instill in you the confidence to settle for nothing less than competent and timely performed legal services, only as needed, and at a fair price.

Barry M. Gallagher

"The good of the people is the chief law."

Cicero

1 Finding the Right Lawyer

Finding a lawyer is not difficult, not when you consider there are some 450,000 lawyers in the United States (approximately one for every 500 people) and some 35,000 more being added to the system each year from law schools around the country. But finding the *right* lawyer can be a difficult task and this is especially so for those who have occasion to need the services of a lawyer only infrequently.

Nearly everyone knows that the right lawyer is one who is competent to perform the needed legal service, does so in a diligent fashion, is honest in his dealings with clients, and charges a reasonable price for those services. Unfortunately, finding and hiring the right lawyer is not as easy as knowing what qualities the right lawyer possesses.

Too often, when faced with a problem demanding the services of a lawyer, people will hire lawyers almost out of desperation, unaware of their rights, with little or no investigation and evaluation of the lawyer hired, and with little more than a hope that the lawyer will perform in a competent manner and at a reasonable cost. The initial feeling of relief in having quickly found a lawyer, and the expectation that the legal problem will soon be solved, can easily give way to feelings of anger and frustration when it is discovered the lawyer hired is not performing as expected.

Whatever the cause, be it a lack of competence on the part of the lawyer, poor communication between lawyer and client, excessive legal fees, promised results never obtained, or any number of other causes, the end result is nearly always the same. The client is unhappy, feels helpless to correct the situation, and feels victimized. Frequently this feeling does not arise until many months after the lawyer has been hired and the client discovers that the lawyer's conduct has resulted in adding to the client's problem, rather than solving it.

The client is then faced with choosing between continuing with the same lawyer or finding a new one. It is not always an easy choice. Few lawyers are anxious to assume responsibility for a client's legal problem after one lawyer has already mishandled that problem. In addition to the time and cost the client incurs in searching for a lawyer to assume such responsibility, the new lawyer must spend valuable time in reviewing what has already been performed by the original lawyer, and in correcting (to the extent possible) his mistakes. All of this adds up to more legal fees than would have been incurred had the client, acting as an informed consumer of legal services, carefully and systematically selected the original lawyer.

To be sure, there is no way to guarantee that the lawyer you hire is right for you and will continue to be right for you. However, by carefully considering whether a particular lawyer possesses certain desired traits, taking the time to carefully consider and investigate various sources of information available to aid you in evaluating the lawyer's ability to meet your legal needs, asking the right questions before you hire the lawyer, knowing your rights as a client once the relationship begins, and in periodically evaluating your lawyer as the relationship proceeds, you can greatly reduce your likelihood of error, and be far more likely to make the right selection the first time.

THE *RIGHT* LAWYER:
A PROFILE

The first step in the process of finding the right lawyer to hire is to consider those traits which are generally thought to be desirable in a lawyer. As we discuss in more detail in Chapter Four, these are not merely traits you hope to find in a lawyer but, rather, traits which you have a right to expect (and obtain) in the lawyer you hire.

Competence

According to a recent study, the primary reason some people with legal needs do not hire lawyers stems from their doubt of the lawyer's competence, and yet, competence in a lawyer must be considered a client's fundamental right.

In a lawyer, competence means a sound legal education, adequate training and experience, and the ability to apply these factors effectively in providing a client with a needed legal service. Such a lawyer is also one who provides that competence on behalf of all his clients and also improves upon his basic legal education and experience through a program of continuing education by means of formal courses as well as independent study.

Integrity

Said to be the very breath of justice, integrity can also be said to be at the very heart of a sound and proper relationship between a lawyer and client. For most people, justice in this country is not that which is administered by judges who see only a small fraction of all legal problems, but that which is found in the offices of lawyers, who advise their various clients on what the law is, how it is applicable to a client's legal problem, and what the lawyer believes the client should do to comply with or avoid that law. Not knowing the law, or how to apply it to a client's legal problem, or giving improper advice on what the client should do in response to such a law can have a disastrous effect on the outcome of the client's legal problem. The uprightness, honesty, and sincerity of the lawyer in providing proper advice is absolutely imperative if the client is to realize the best that our system of justice can offer.

Judgment

Some people dislike making decisions and there are lawyers among that group. That the lawyer you hire has the ability to make a decision, and that he do so only after comparing and deciding among all alternatives, is necessary if you are to receive the best legal advice. The judgment of the lawyer you hire may well affect your money, your property, your future, or even your life, and the advice must be solid and capable of being depended upon.

Dedication

A truly dedicated lawyer is one who is motivated not merely to do the minimum required to perform the client's needed legal service, but all that which is required to properly protect the client's interest. Such a lawyer will apply this dedication equally to the poor and oppressed, as well as to those clients who can afford to pay for the lawyer's services. Many lawyers profess such dedication to the practice of law and the needs of their clients, but not all exhibit it by their actions.

"There are three sorts of lawyers — able, unable, lamentable."

Robert Smith Surtees
Plain or Ringlet?

Maturity

As with all endeavors, those who engage in the practice of law can develop and grow into ever more capable lawyers by the application of law school training and knowledge to actual client problems and involvement in the administration of justice. Such activities provide an opportunity for a lawyer to more fully develop his abilities and effectiveness in providing needed legal services and the self-reliance which follows.

Compassion

Although sometimes thought of as cold and calculating individuals who act with indifference to the problems of their clients, most lawyers who obtain a high degree of excellence in reputation do so because of their ability to understand a client's legal problem, to deal with the ramifications of that problem as it effects the client, and to be patient in relating to the client.

THE IMPORTANT INTANGIBLE: 17
HOW YOU FEEL ABOUT THE LAWYER

Even a lawyer possessed of all the traits discussed above may not be the right lawyer for you. There is an additional but intangible factor too often overlooked by a person searching for a lawyer. This important factor is how you *feel* about the lawyer under consideration.

A feeling of discomfort about a lawyer, which may not be readily apparent nor easily understood, poses a serious threat to the relationship between a lawyer and client. Not infrequently, clients who end up in a dispute with the lawyers they hired recall only too late having felt uncomfortable about the lawyer or in something the lawyer said or did. For one reason or another, the client fails to adequately consider such a feeling, or chooses to overlook the feeling, and proceeds to hire the lawyer. This can be a costly mistake.

By its very nature, the relationship between a lawyer and client is a close and personal one in which the client must have the ability to confer candidly with the lawyer selected, rely on the lawyer's judgment and advice, and trust that lawyer fully. These are the essentials to a sound relationship between a lawyer and client. If your doubt about the lawyer persists, even though you can only explain it as a "feeling" and not otherwise, find and hire another lawyer.

BEGINNING YOUR SEARCH
FOR THE RIGHT LAWYER

Various studies have indicated a substantial majority of all those who hire lawyers do so on the recommendation of a friend or relative. As a starting point in your search for the right lawyer, consulting a friend or relative is fine. But without a good deal of additional information, it is little better than picking a lawyer's name at random from your local telephone directory.

If you are to make an informed choice about which among various lawyers in the community you should hire, it is necessary to know what alternative sources of information are available by which to obtain the names of such lawyers and to acquire information pertaining to them which you need if your choice is to truly be an informed one.

Friends, Relatives, and Associates

If you intend to rely on the recommendation of a friend, relative, or associate, as to which lawyer you should consult for your legal needs, be sure you ask the following questions:

- Have you ever used the lawyer to whom you are referring me?
- Do you know someone who has used this lawyer?

It is important that you distinguish between being referred to a lawyer by a person who has actually used that lawyer and being referred to a lawyer simply because someone has heard of him.

- What can you tell me about this lawyer?

If your friend, relative, or associate knows the type of law practice in which the lawyer engages, the names of some of his clients, his usual fee arrangement, and the like, you will then have some information with which to determine if a meeting with that lawyer should be arranged. Chapter Three contains a detailed discussion of how you should conduct such a meeting and what information you should obtain from the lawyer before deciding whether to hire him.

Lawyer Advertising

For many years, a majority of the members of the legal profession were successful in their opposition to advertising by lawyers. But a recent United States Supreme Court ruling has finally overcome such opposition. Now, lawyers are beginning to advertise in newspapers, on radios and television, and in various circulars and brochures. As a source for obtaining the name, address and telephone number of a lawyer, and in some instances the field of law in which the lawyer is primarily engaged, such advertising is indeed helpful. But you should not rely on an advertisement by a lawyer as an alternative to your own thorough evaluation of the lawyer behind the advertisement.

Contrary to the belief of some lawyers that advertising can be a shortcut method to building a law practice, there is no substitute for an adequate legal education, proper training and experience, and the earned reputation for excellence which a lawyer can only acquire by exhibiting competence and fair dealings over a substantial period of time. If you are considering whether to hire a lawyer whose advertisement has come to your attention, ask yourself the following questions:

- Why is the lawyer advertising his services?

Perhaps the lawyer, as a gesture of public service, wishes to make known the availability of his legal services. But more likely, the lawyer wants to get new business and if this is so, you must be concerned about whether the lawyer is unable to get such business in the traditional manner based on a reputation for excellence.

- What does the advertisement really tell me?
- Does the advertisement indicate a particular field of law in which the lawyer is primarily engaged?

It may not be commonly known, but some lawyers hire professional advertising agencies and public relation firms to help promote their business. In some instances, such firms are hired to carefully prepare advertisements that literally attempt to "sell" the lawyer as willing and able to provide you with the legal service you need. While such advertisements will tell you much about the skill of the people who prepare them, they frequently tell you little or nothing about the lawyer's training, experience, and skill. As in other forms of commercials on television and radio advertising services, the "lawyer" in the advertisement may well be an actor playing his part solely to get your legal business. It is up to you to see that your business goes only to someone qualified to perform the service you need. In considering a lawyer's advertisement, look for the following:

- Is a fee schedule mentioned?

In some advertisements by lawyers, reference is made to a fee schedule which is available on request or in the lawyer's office. If you see such an advertisement, be sure you ask for and receive a fee schedule. You may wish to refer to it later, in the event you hire the lawyer and a dispute concerning legal fees arises.

■ Is the cost of the first meeting with the lawyer indicated?   21

If so, you will know in advance the cost of meeting with the lawyer to determine whether he is right for you.

■ Is a copy or transcript of the advertisement available?

If you intend to hire a lawyer who came to your attention through an advertisement, insist that the lawyer provide you with a copy or transcript of the advertisement. In this way, you will have a record of what the lawyer represented with regard to his services, fees, and ability, to the extent the advertisement makes mention of these.

Legal Aid Services

Legal Aid Services is a general term used to indicate those offices, societies, and organizations that have been established to assist the poor in meeting their legal needs. Funded by the federal government and each state, they exist in hundreds of locations throughout the United States. Operated on limited budgets, they are not recommended as referral sources unless you are, in fact, eligible for such assistance. Most legal aid offices are listed in the phone book, but your local or state bar association (See Appendix B) will also be able to direct you to the legal aid service office near where you live to determine if you qualify for such assistance. (A more detailed explanation of the services provided by such offices is contained in Chapter Two.)

Lawyer Referral Services

Established in response to the public's need for assistance in finding a lawyer, these services exist throughout the United

States. Many operate under the direction or control of local or state bar associations. Some provide excellent referral services by making available a lawyer or other trained individual to conduct the initial interview with the person using the service and then referring that person to a lawyer predetermined to have both the capability and the willingness to provide the needed legal service. Other and less desirable services operate on a straight rotation basis, merely giving the person using the service the name of the next available lawyer on a referral list and with no evaluation of the person's needs or the skills of the lawyer to whom that person is referred.

If you intend to use a lawyer referral service, be sure you ask the following questions:

- Is there a fee for using the service?

Many services charge a nominal fee, such as $10 or $15, for use of the service. Such a fee is intended to offset the cost of operating the service.

- Who operates the service?
- How are lawyers selected for membership on the referral list?

By knowing who operates the service you should be able to determine whether it is truly an effort as a public service to provide you with assistance, or is merely designed to bring clients to those lawyers otherwise unable to develop an active law practice. If membership of the referral list requires only the payment of a fee by the lawyer, with no effort made to evaluate the lawyer who requests such membership, the use of the service is nothing more than the random selection of a lawyer and is equally as bad.

- Will I be interviewed before being referred to a lawyer?
- What effort will be made to refer me to a lawyer with special expertise in the field of law to which my problem relates?

The better operated services conduct an initial interview to insure that the person using the service will be matched with a lawyer who has not only expressed willingness to participate in the service, but who is also qualified to provide the needed legal service.

- What information can you provide me about the lawyer to whom I am being referred?

If the service provides you with nothing more than a lawyer's name, telephone number, and address, the service is not being properly operated.

- Will I be charged for the initial interview with the lawyer to whom I am being referred?
- If so, how much?

Some services, as a condition to adding a lawyer's name to the referral list, require the lawyer to agree to a minimal and fixed cost for the initial interview with anyone referred by the service.

- If I hire the lawyer to whom I am referred, and a dispute subsequently arises, will the service provide assistance in resolving the dispute?

The better services not only monitor the performance of lawyers referred by the service, they also provide assistance in resolving any dispute which may arise between a lawyer on the list and a person referred by the service of that lawyer.

Look in your local telephone directory for the address and telephone number for the service nearest you, or call the local or state bar association where you live for assistance in locating the nearest service. For more information on these services, and how such a service can be started in your community, write to the American Bar Association, Standing Committee On Lawyer Referral Services, 1155 East 60th Street, Chicago, Illinois, 60637, (312) 947-3673.

Professional Advisors

This source includes such people as accountants, bankers, insurance agents, and real estate brokers. Because of the nature of their own business activities, they frequently have contact with lawyers in the community or with clients of those lawyers. Many of the individuals in this category are in a position to provide you with information on the lawyer's past or present financial dealings, his reputation in the community, and the names of some of his clients, all valuable information in evaluating the lawyer to whom you are referred.

Legal Clinics

A relatively recent development in the practice of law, these "clinics" are designed to handle large volumes of routine legal work at reduced rates resulting from the utilization of standardized forms, procedures and interviewing techniques; non-lawyer assistants; programmed typewriters; and similar time-and-money-saving devices. Be- cause they are dependent on a high volume of legal business, such clinics are seldom adequate to provide needed services for substantial or complex legal problems and are generally not the place to look for a lawyer with special skills, or for a referral to such a lawyer.

Directories and Other Lawyer Lists

Unknown to most non-lawyers, there are numerous directories and lists which contain the names, addresses, and telephone numbers of lawyers. Some provide little information about a lawyer other than that which is available in a telephone directory. Others, such as the Martindale-Hubbell Law Directory, published by Martindale-Hubbell, Inc., contain a wealth of information on listed lawyers, including, in many instances, the educational background of those lawyers, their professional activities and fields of law practice, and the identity of some of their clients. Most such directories and lists are available in city and county law libraries throughout the United States as well as those maintained by law schools. In addition, many lawyers have one or more of these directories or lists available in their office.

Company and Union Legal Representative

You may work for a company or belong to a union with a lawyer on its staff or a representative who acts as a liaison with a lawyer in private practice. If so, consider this person as a source for assistance in finding a lawyer and be sure to ask the following questions in consulting him:

■ What can you tell me about the lawyer to whom you are referring me?

Find out if you are being referred to a lawyer who is known to the person making the referral. It may merely be a company or union policy to refer individuals to a particular lawyer and the person making the referral may merely be complying with such policy, without any firsthand knowledge about the lawyer.

■ Have you referred other people to this lawyer?

This question is designed to provide you with information which you can subsequently verify as to the satisfaction or dissatisfaction of others who have been referred to the same lawyer. By getting the names of these people, you may be able to make convenient contact with them at your place of work or the next union meeting.

■ What is the lawyer's usual fee arrangement?
■ Will I be charged for the first meeting?

Answers to these questions will assist you in evaluating what the person making the referral actually knows about the lawyer, as well as what you can expect in the way of a charge for the first meeting with the lawyer to whom you are referred.

■ Will you receive a fee or anything else for referring me to the lawyer?

Obviously, if the person making the referral is receiving a fee, he may be more inclined to refer you to a lawyer willing to pay such a fee than to a lawyer who is both capable and willing to provide the legal service you need.

Other Excellent Sources

In addition to the above more or less standard means of finding the lawyer who is right for you, there are some other means which are, perhaps, a little less standard but are nevertheless excellent sources for finding lawyers of recognized ability.

Judges and Other Courthouse Personnel

Because they have an excellent opportunity to observe many lawyers in their day-to-day practice, and particularly to observe those lawyers who engage in trial work and probate matters, judges can be an excellent source of information on finding a lawyer. Although many judges are busy and spend a good portion of their workday in court, you may be able to contact a judge by telephone. Even if you are unable to do so, you should be able to reach the judge's clerk or assistant and ask that person to inquire of the judge, on your behalf, for assistance in finding a good lawyer.

In addition to judges, there are other courthouse personnel, such as clerks, secretaries, and court reporters, who also have an excellent opportunity to observe and come to know many lawyers and evaluate those lawyers in terms of timeliness, preparation, presentation, effectiveness, and similar qualities. They too can provide you with assistance.

City and County Law Libraries

Many cities and most counties throughout the United States maintain law libraries for use by local government officials such as judges, public prosecutors, and city and county employees. Generally, lawyers in the community are also free to use the library. The librarian and his assistants are usually in frequent contact with such lawyers and representatives of local legal service organizations who also use the library, and as such are in a position to provide you with assistance in finding the right lawyer. They can also assist you in using the directories and other lawyer lists mentioned above, which the library should have.

Law Schools

Some law schools provide a referral service to assist people in finding a lawyer. Even among those schools which do not, members of the administration or faculty are usually available to provide such assistance. Because of the relatively small size of most law schools when compared with most colleges, it is not uncommon for members of the administration or faculty to stay in contact with former students after they become lawyers. Having observed such lawyers in their student days, they are in an excellent position to provide you with good referrals.

In addition, some schools conduct continuing legal education courses for practicing lawyers in the community and, to the extent members of the administration or faculty of the school participate in such courses, they tend to know and evaluate those lawyers who have exhibited an interest in continuing their legal education and are keeping abreast of current developments in the law. The same is true of a faculty member who teaches in a particular field of law to which your legal need relates. He is likely to know a number of lawyers in the community who practice in the same field of law and should be able to assist you in finding the right lawyer.

Stenographic
Shorthand Reporters

Although also known as court reporters, this category of reporters is intended to refer to those free-lance reporters who do not work in a courtroom but, rather, are hired by lawyers to take sworn statements from parties and witnesses to lawsuits, and prepare transcripts of hearings relating to legal matters. In doing so, they have an excellent opportunity to observe and compare many lawyers, particularly those lawyers who engage in lawsuit-related matters, and come to know which lawyers are consistently prepared and regularly perform in a competent fashion. For the name, address, and telephone number of a reporter in your community, consult your local telephone directory under the listing "Reporters—Court And Convention" or some similar listing.

Military Legal
Assistance Offices

If you are a member of the Armed Forces, or a dependent of a member, you are probably eligible for legal assistance from a lawyer on active military service duty. Contact the legal assistance officer where you are stationed or nearest to where you reside and inquire as to what legal assistance is available. Even if your need requires a civilian lawyer, the legal assistance officer can help you select the right lawyer.

GENERAL PRACTITIONER
OR LEGAL SPECIALIST?

In addition to considering what professional qualifications you desire in the lawyer you will hire, you must also consider whether to hire a *general practitioner* who provides legal services in a number of fields of law, or a *legal specialist* who limits his practice to a particular field of law so as to develop and maintain special expertise.

It is clear the trend is toward more and more specialization among lawyers. This is attributable to a number of factors including the sheer effort required to develop adequate knowledge of the subject matter and keep abreast of new developments in only one or two fields of law, the natural tendency of law firm lawyers to gravitate to a particular field of law in which they enjoy and to develop special expertise in that field, and the ever-increasing demand of clients that lawyers exhibit not only competence, but attention to economy. Legal counsel can be provided most economically by a lawyer with the special expertise necessary to most efficiently perform the service required.

For many years, as this trend has developed, members of the organized legal profession and others have debated the issue of specialization as it affects the profession, members of the public, and individual lawyers. Some feel specialization poses a threat to the influence and even the existence of the organized legal profession because of the tendency of lawyer specialists to form special interest groups which are not necessarily for the betterment of the profession as a whole. Others feel the public is best served by lawyers able to provide a full range of legal services to a client and who possess the peripheral vision necessary for the effective representation of a client with separate but overlapping personal, family, and business legal needs. Still others express alarm at the thought of lawyers developing a tendency, through specialization, to be overly narrow in their view of the law and its applicability to a client's needs.

RECOGNIZED FIELDS OF LAW

Administrative
Adoptions
Agriculture
Antitrust
Aviation
Banking
Bankruptcy
Civil Rights
Commercial
Communications
Computer
Constitution
Consumer
Contracts
Copyright
Corporate
Criminal
Education
Entertainment
Environment
Estate Planning/Wills
Family Law
Governmental

Health
Immigration/Naturalization
Insurance
International
Juvenile
Labor
Landlord/Tenant
Maritime
Military
Mortgage
Natural Resources
Negligence
Patents/Trademarks
Probate
Real Property
Securities
Social Security
Taxation
Transportation
Trusts
Utilities
Workmen's Compensation

32   Other issues involving specialization are: whether such specialization should begin with training in law school or at some later point in a lawyer's career, the best way to recognize and certify specialists, how the public can thus be protected against lawyers who falsely claim the status of a specialist, the tendency of general practitioners not to refer clients to specialists because of the fear of losing such clients, concern that lawyers who specialize will be less responsible to clients since their legal advice may be limited only to a particular part of a client's overall legal needs, and whether a lawyer who is a specialist in one field of law should be permitted to practice in other fields in which he is not a specialist.

No doubt some of the opposition to specialization is well-meaning and many of the issues raised are still unresolved. But when one considers the large number of generally recognized fields of law, as listed above, and the fact that even within each of these fields are numerous sub-fields which are themselves frequently the subject of specialization, it becomes readily apparent that no one lawyer can hope to maintain adequate proficiency in all or even a few fields of law.

THE ADVANTAGES OF
A SPECIALIST

Improved Quality of
Legal Services

A legal specialist, by concentrating his training, experience, and continuing education on a limited field of law, can almost always provide superior legal services to those provided by a general practitioner. A lawyer who devotes all or substantially all of his time and attention to a particular field of law, or providing a particular legal service, will generally know that field of law better and perform that service in a more competent fashion than will a lawyer whose time and attention is spread over various services among many fields of law.

Reduce Cost of
Legal Services

Although many specialists charge a higher rate per hour, most are able to perform a particular service with more efficiency than a general practitioner. This usually means they perform the service in less time, and, despite the higher cost per hour for the lawyer's time, the cost to you is frequently less than that which you would pay to a general practitioner.

Better Access to
the Right Lawyer

A few states, in an effort to recognize and make known the special expertise or skills of some lawyers, have established, or are considering the establishment of formal programs for the certification or designation of such lawyers, who are then free to make known to the public their area of specialization as recognized by the state in which they practice.

But you should not be misled into believing that only those lawyers who receive formal certification or designation can truly be considered specialists. For in both those states with formal certification or designation programs, and the many states without such programs, there are many, many lawyers who are in fact specialists. The true test of a specialist is not the meeting of formal requirements but, rather, the lawyer's knowledge and expertise in a particular field of law. Do not rely on some "proof" of formal certification or designation as a specialist, or some claim to such status by the lawyer. As suggested in Chapter Three, determine to your own satisfaction that the lawyer is truly a specialist in the field of law to which your legal problem relates.

SOLO PRACTITIONER OR LAW FIRM LAWYER?

Approximately one-half of all lawyers in private practice in the United States are solo practitioners, as distinguished from the other one-half who are members of law firms made up of from two to twenty or more lawyers. Because of this, your search for the right lawyer will probably require you to choose between these two types of lawyers.

Your choice will not be an easy one. There are no hard and fast rules to guide you and there are advantages and disadvantages to hiring either type. Failure to recognize your alternatives and to carefully consider your choice can greatly affect the quality of the legal service you receive, the cost of that service, and the outcome of the legal problem you face.

Because our system of legal education is engaged primarily in teaching law students the principles of law, they are likely to have no experience, prior to becoming lawyers, in applying those principles to real client problems. As newly admitted lawyers, they are free to go directly into solo practice, or join a law firm.

For those who join a law firm, experience usually comes under the watchful eye of a more senior lawyer within the firm. In this way the new lawyer avoids the trial-and-error method which his counterpart, who has gone directly into solo practice, is very likely to experience. Not infrequently, the mistakes made by a newly admitted lawyer in solo practice are paid for by his clients.

Not all solo practitioners, however, are newly admitted to the practice of law. Many are mature, experienced, capable lawyers who once worked for a law firm, and, for any number of reasons, left that firm to practice law alone. It is because of this that you must carefully weigh the advantages and disadvantages of choosing between an experienced solo practitioner and a law firm lawyer. What follows is a discussion of some of these advantages and disadvantages.

Nature of Problem

Your legal need will likely be a major factor in choosing between a solo practitioner and a law firm lawyer. While a solo practitioner will generally handle an individual's legal problems, and those of a family nature, a law firm lawyer will handle these problems plus those of a more complex nature involving business matters and the like. The reason for this is that a group of lawyers collected together in a law firm are better able to provide the various legal services required for the more complex legal needs.

Accessibility

Depending on where you live, your choice between a solo practitioner and a law firm lawyer may be somewhat restricted. While solo practitioners exist in nearly every community, law firms tend to be more prevalent in the more urban areas.

Responsiveness

Although both the solo practitioner and law firm lawyer can be equally responsive to a client's needs, the solo practitioner may be more inclined to maintain that responsiveness than a law firm lawyer. This is due to the fact that most law firms have numerous clients and therefore tend to be less dependent on any single one. The sheer size of some law firms creates a degree of impersonality not found as frequently among solo practitioners. But in another sense, a law firm lawyer may be better able to respond quickly to your legal needs. This is due to the fact that nearly all law firms have greater staff support than do solo practitioners.

Legal Costs

Generally, a solo practitioner will have fewer overhead expenses than will a law firm lawyer. The reason for this is that as the number of lawyers within the firm increases, the cost of providing the necessary office space, staff support, and other facilities required for the successful operation of the law office increases dramatically. This means that many times a solo practitioner will charge less than a law firm lawyer for the same legal service.

Specialization

Within a law firm, there tends to be a natural allocation of legal services according to each individual lawyer's intelligence, training, experience, motivation, ambition, and personality. Where one lawyer within the firm may exhibit great interest and ability in performing trial work, another may detest trial work but enjoy and excel at performing real estate-related services, whereas another may prefer tax-related matters. A solo practitioner, on the other hand, may be requested to perform services in each of these areas of law. Therefore, he will generally not have the same opportunity to develop the special skill and expertise which a law firm lawyer, who can focus his energies and efforts to a particular field of law or legal skill, can acquire. However, there are solo practitioners who limit their practice to a particular field of law or legal skill and thus become specialists.

Work Load

An active law practice can be just as taxing on a law firm lawyer as on a solo practitioner. A law firm lawyer, however, usually enjoys greater staff support and the invaluable opportunity to readily consult with and obtain the advice of fellow lawyers within the law firm. One has only to imagine a solo practitioner engaged daily on behalf of only one client in a trial lasting many weeks to realize that during such a trial the needs of other clients may go unmet. In a similar situation, a law firm lawyer can refer a client with a pressing legal problem to a fellow lawyer within the law firm. The solo practitioner may be reluctant to make such a referral as it may mean losing the client.

Staff Support

While most solo practitioners employ a secretary, and some even employ one or more assistants for research and other functions related to providing legal services, many law firms not only employ secretaries, but also employ paralegals, research clerks, and others who act as staff support. Such additional staff support generally gives a law firm lawyer a better opportunity to meet the demands and needs of those clients who are faced with legal problems that require immediate attention.

Research Facilities

Almost always, a law firm lawyer will have better access to legal research facilities than will a sole practitioner. Most law firms maintain sizable law libraries which are required both by the number of lawyers within the firm, and the type of legal services which most law firms provide. The larger law firms even employ librarians and other library-related assistants to maintain the library and to provide the lawyers of the firm with assistance in research and other client-related needs. Many law firms also maintain files of various forms for contracts, leases, and other agreements, as well as legal research memorandums—all of which are available to the lawyer members of the firm with the aim of saving time and expense in meeting a client's particular need.

Financial Responsibility

Although many solo practitioners are as financially responsible as law firm lawyers, the client of a law firm has that firm's additional financial protection should the client suffer and claim damage because of legal malpractice. In some instances, however, what appears to be a law firm is really

nothing more than a collection of solo practitioners who
have joined together to share office space, secretarial assistance, and so on. Sometimes the solo practitioners will use
a common letterhead on their stationery, and even the same
address and telephone number. If in doubt about the status
of a particular lawyer's relationship to what appears to be a
law firm, you should ask the following questions:

- Are the lawyers in this office all members of a partnership?
- Are you a member of that partnership?

Continuity of
Representation

The unexpected illness or injury of a solo practitioner can
leave his clients in a most difficult position. But the client of
a law firm lawyer, when faced with a similar situation, is
much less likely to suffer damage. This is due to the fact that
fellow lawyers within the law firm can temporarily fill in or
replace the ill or injured lawyer and permit the client to
avoid having to change lawyers before completion of the
needed legal service.

Full Legal Service

If you operate a business, or have other repeated needs for
legal services, a law firm will almost always be better able
to provide the needed services. Because law firm lawyers
tend to develop special areas of practice within a law firm,
they are better able to meet the varied needs of a client
who, on one occasion, may need advice on the purchase of
real property, and on another, need assistance in the preparation of a will or trust.

40 When considering whether to hire a particular lawyer, it is best to be able to compare that lawyer with other lawyers. In order to do this, it is suggested that you obtain the names of at least two and preferably three lawyers with whom you will want to meet and discuss your legal needs. Chapter Three contains information to assist you in evaluating each of the lawyers before deciding whom to hire. A significant part of that evaluation will relate to the matter of legal fees and the cost of obtaining the needed service, which is discussed in Chapter Two.

2 Legal Fees: What You Should Know

Excessive legal fees are recognized as a major cause of breakdown in lawyer/client relationships. Client complaints range from mild concern to outright anger and disbelief. Many of these complaints can be traced to the failure of a lawyer and a client to have a full and frank discussion regarding legal fees at the outset of the relationship.

The causes of this failure are many. In some instances, a client receives an unrealistic appraisal of what he can expect in the way of legal fees because of an inexperienced lawyer's inability to properly assess the client's legal problem or the cost of its solution. In other instances, the lawyer may be so intent upon obtaining the prospective client's business that he fails to fully apprise the client of what can be expected in the way of legal fees. In still other instances, a poorly drafted fee agreement, usually prepared by the lawyer, may mislead the client, and ultimately cause the relationship to break down. When this happens, it is the client who is most likely to feel frustrated, not know what action to take, and feel helpless to negotiate a resolution to the dispute with the lawyer.

The importance and benefit of a full and frank discussion about legal fees before you hire a lawyer can not be overemphasized. Far too many people in need of legal services hire a lawyer knowing little more than the lawyer's hourly rate or the percentage by which the lawyer's contingent fee will be computed. Lack of adequate knowledge and information about legal fees, feelings of embarrassment about discussing legal fees with a lawyer, or the incorrect belief that a client has little or no control over legal fees, usually mean the client is going to have a dispute with his lawyer over such fees. To avoid such a dispute with a lawyer, you must understand and be prepared to discuss the subject of legal fees before deciding whether to hire that lawyer.

"Lawyers are as professional as your aunt's eye. They are businessmen, engaged in a decidedly bottom-line business. They give you advice and they charge you for it."

Charles McCabe
San Francisco Chronicle

TYPES OF LEGAL FEES

Generally speaking, legal fees can be classified by type into one of the following categories:

Hourly Fee

If the lawyer will receive compensation for services rendered based on a dollar amount per hour, the fee is commonly referred to as an hourly fee. For example, if a lawyer is charging $60 per hour and takes 18 minutes to draft a letter on behalf of a client, the client's cost for those legal services will be $18.

Many lawyers maintain a written record of the time expended in providing each legal service to each client. If the lawyer keeps an accurate record of the time he expends, an hourly fee arrangement means the client pays only for the services actually rendered by the lawyer. But if the lawyer is required to expend substantial time in providing a needed legal service, an hourly fee arrangement may prove a disadvantage to a client since the greater amount of time the lawyer is required to expend on the client's behalf, the greater the legal fee to the client. In instances where a client is involved in lengthy litigation, such a fee arrangement can result in a long series of monthly or other periodic billing statements requiring the payment of substantial legal fees before the outcome of the litigation is known.

Contingent Fee

When a lawyer's compensation depends upon the successful outcome of the client's legal matter, the fee is often referred to as a contingent fee. In such cases, the client is only obligated to pay the lawyer for services rendered if a favorable judgment or settlement occurs.

A contingent fee arrangement occurs most frequently where a lawyer is hired to pursue a client's claim for damages, and the client does not wish to, or is unable to pay the lawyer on an hourly basis for the time the lawyer expends in pursuing the claim. Typically, a lawyer is willing to perform the legal service on a contingent fee basis because of his belief that he will be successful in pursuing the client's claim and will be able to share in the recovery sum paid to the client.

The advantage to the client in a contingent fee arrangement
is immediately apparent. If the lawyer is unsuccessful in
pursuing the client's claim, there is no obligation to pay the
lawyer for his services. What is not so apparent is the unfortunate practice among some lawyers of failing to
adequately investigate the merits of a client's claim before
agreeing to a contingent fee arrangement. When the lawyer
subsequently learns the claim has less value than was originally estimated, or discovers that substantially more work
is involved in pursuing the client's claim than was originally
estimated, the lawyer may lose interest in the vigorous pursuit of the claim to the detriment of the client. Such a loss of
interest is many times difficult to detect, and even when
detected, the client faces a difficult task of finding another
lawyer willing to accept the case on a contingent fee basis
after one lawyer has begun, but not completed, the matter.

On some occasions, lawyers have been criticized for accepting matters on a contingent fee basis because they have
obtained a so-called "windfall." By this is meant that the
lawyer receives substantially more money for the service he
provides than would have been the case had he been com-
pensated on an hourly basis. But to a client with limited
funds, a contingent fee basis may be the only way in which
the client can pursue a valid claim and hope to recover for
damages incurred.

If you are concerned about the lawyer you hire receiving a
"windfall," consider various fee arrangements available,
obtain an estimate of the amount of the fee likely to be
incurred depending on the type of fee arrangement you
select, and discuss the matter in detail with each lawyer
you consider for employment, before deciding on a particular fee arrangement and lawyer.

If you do enter into a contingent fee arrangement, be sure you understand how the contingent fee will be determined. *The lawyer's contingent fee should be computed only on the basis of the net recovery, not the gross recovery.* Any costs which you have incurred in pursuing the claim should be reimbursed to you and deducted from the total amount recovered, before the lawyer's contingent fee is determined from the balance of the recovery.

You should also be aware that some states prohibit contingent fees in certain types of legal matters and place a maximum limit on the amount a lawyer can recover on a contingent fee basis in other types of cases.

Flat Fee

Because of the routine nature of some legal services provided by lawyers, such as the preparation of a simple will or the drafting of a simple contract document, lawyers sometimes quote and agree to a flat, or stated amount, fee for performing the service. To a client, the advantage is obvious since he knows in advance what the total legal fee will be for the completed service. However, if the lawyer mistakenly estimates the amount of time required to perform the service, the client may get less than competent performance if the lawyer hurries the work to meet his own estimate. Also, there is the possibility that a lawyer will request an increase in the fee in order to compensate for his erroneous estimate. In some rare instances, renegotiating a fee arrangement after the lawyer has agreed to undertake the client's representation may be required by the occurrence of an unexpected event. But from the client's standpoint, such a request by a lawyer should be viewed with suspicion and the lawyer should be able to fully justify any such request for modification of the originally quoted fee. An experienced lawyer is usually able to correctly estimate the amount of time necessary to perform a given service, and thus be able to quote a realistic flat fee at the outset of the relationship.

In some instances, a flat fee is paid in segments. By this it is meant that the lawyer receives a specified amount for performing a part of the client's needed legal service to an agreed upon point. If the lawyer continues to provide additional services, such as going beyond the stage of negotiating the client's claim, and is required to file and prepare a lawsuit for trial, the lawyer receives an additional fee. If the matter proceeds to trial, the lawyer may receive still another fee on completion of the trial and the same may be true if an appeal is taken for which the lawyer represents the client.

Percentage Fee

Laws applicable to the performance of some legal services provide that the lawyer handling them is to be paid a percentage of the total value of the assets for which he is responsible during the performance of the service. Typically, a lawyer will receive such a percentage fee when probating an estate or acting as legal counsel to the executor of an estate. Another example is when a lawyer acts as a court-appointed receiver and is paid a percentage of cash disbursements and receipts.

Retainer Fee

In some instances, to insure the continuous availability of a lawyer or law firm, a client will agree to pay a monthly or yearly retainer fee. Such a fee is normally paid to insure the performance of legal services for ongoing, routine legal needs. Normally a retainer fee is agreed upon as fair compensation for all specified work to be performed within a given period and with the provision that the lawyer or law firm receiving such a fee will receive additional compensation for rendering legal services not considered routine or within the terms of the retainer agreement. But if the agreement is not carefully drafted, confusion may arise over what constitutes an extraordinary or non-routine legal service for which additional fees, over and above the retainer fee, are incurred.

FACTORS DETERMINING LEGAL FEES: THE LAWYER'S CONSIDERATIONS

In considering what fee arrangement to propose to a prospective client, most lawyers will consider some or all of the following factors:

Nature of the Needed Legal Service

Viewed from the standpoint of a client, a legal problem may appear overwhelming. That same legal problem, when viewed from the standpoint of a lawyer, may appear routine in nature and easily handled, based on the lawyer's knowledge of the applicable law and his training and experience in handling similar problems. If the matter is a routine one, the lawyer is likely to charge a lesser fee than he might if he viewed the problem, and the needed legal service to solve that problem, as unique or highly unusual in its complexity and requiring extensive research, preparation, consultation with others, travel, or additional office staffing.

Reputation of
the Lawyer

Generally, the more famous the lawyer, the greater the fee which that lawyer can command. If a lawyer is known as a legal specialist, or one otherwise having special expertise in the handling of a certain type of legal problem, or in providing a certain legal service, he may well be in great demand and able to command a greater fee than a lawyer of lesser reputation.

Amount Involved

Lawyers, like many others, tend to be attracted to matters involving substantial sums of money. The greater the amount involved in a legal problem, the more likely it is to attract competent lawyers. And such lawyers are likely to charge greater fees because of the amount involved in the problem, their own level of competency, the increased responsibility in providing the legal service, and the extra effort and caution required.

Workload of
the Lawyer

Consideration of this factor includes not only the lawyer's time in providing the services required by other clients, but also the lawyer's office staff capabilities. If, by accepting the offered employment, the lawyer will be required to add to his existing staff, or might have to turn away other business because of the increased workload, he may wish to charge a fee consistent with these considerations.

"A lawyer's time and advice is his stock in trade."

Abraham Lincoln

Relationship with the Client

If the needed service is viewed as the beginning of what is likely to be an ongoing relationship between the lawyer and the client, or the continuation of an existing relationship, a lawyer is likely to charge a lesser fee than he might with a one-time client. The degree of difficulty in communication and cooperation between the lawyer and the client in past dealings may also affect the fee consideration.

Nature or Type of Fee

For a lawyer just beginning to develop his own practice, an hourly fee arrangement may be most desirable since it will assure income, usually on a monthly basis, during the time required to provide the needed service. For a more established, financially secure lawyer, a contingent fee may be more desirable since it provides the opportunity to recover substantially more than might otherwise be earned on an hourly basis.

Total Estimated Fee

Few lawyers agree to a particular fee arrangement without first estimating the total fee likely to be earned in providing the needed service. If the client finds the total estimated fee to be excessive, the lawyer may be agreeable to a lesser hourly charge or a reduced share based on a contingent fee arrangement.

Ability of
the Client to Pay

For some lawyers, a client's ability to pay is considered in determining what fee to charge. Obviously, a client with substantial net worth may pay more for the same legal service than will a client with a lesser net worth.

Successful Result

Where a lawyer has been particularly successful in securing a favorable result for a client, and the lawyer and client agreed that the fee would be determined after the completion of the lawyer's services, the lawyer may take his success into consideration in determining what fee to charge the client.

AN IMPORTANT FACT TO REMEMBER:
LEGAL FEES ARE NEGOTIABLE

For many years, lawyers referred to a minimum fee schedules published by local or state bar associations to determine what fee to quote a prospective client in performing a legal service listed on the schedule. Any lawyer who failed to adhere to the schedule was subject to disciplinary action. However, in 1975, the United States Supreme Court held the practice of requiring lawyers to adhere to minimum fee schedules was an illegal restraint on trade in legal services which had the effect of keeping the cost of such services artificially high.

Although minimum fee schedules are no longer utilized by lawyers, and there are certain maximum limits to what a lawyer may receive as compensation in certain types of legal matters, many clients fail to recognize that legal fees are negotiable. They simply accept whatever the lawyer with whom they are meeting proposes as a fee arrangement.

Remember, you are the one paying for the legal service which you need. While there may be laws which place a maximum on what a lawyer can charge for a particular legal service, there is no minimum and you should not hesitate to negotiate a fee arrangement which you feel is fair. This may mean "shopping" for the best fee arrangement and you should not hesitate to do so. Just as in purchasing an automobile, looking for a home, or making any other substantial purchase, it is usually worth your while to take the time necessary to determine that the amount you pay is fair in relation to your ability to pay, your needs, and the quality of service you receive in return.

ADDITIONAL COSTS TO CONSIDER
BEFORE HIRING A LAWYER

It is common for most clients, before deciding to hire a lawyer, to make some estimate of the total legal fees likely to be incurred in obtaining the needed legal service. Unfortunately, many clients fail to consider costs other than legal fees which are likely to be incurred. When these costs subsequently arise, they create hardship or form the basis for a dispute between the lawyer and the client.

Undoubtedly, lawsuits are the most common type of legal problem in which costs over and above legal fees crop up. Typical of such costs are investigative reports, medical reports, expert witness fees, non-expert witness fees, various court charges related to the filing and recording of legal documents, charges for services of legal process, subpoena fees, travel expenses, photocopying costs, and printing charges.

While it is difficult in many cases to know in advance what the total dollar amount of such costs will be, the nature of the legal problem will usually provide an experienced lawyer with a basis for making a reasonably accurate estimate of the total dollar amount of such costs likely to be incurred. The point to be made here is to fully discuss such costs with the lawyer you are considering hiring and to include these costs when estimating the total cost to you of obtaining the needed legal service.

FEE SPLITTING AND
REFERRAL FEES AMONG LAWYERS

Some lawyers engage in the practice of convincing clients to sign fee agreements with them and then refer those clients to some other lawyer who actually performs the needed legal service. The referring lawyer then receives some portion of the legal fee earned by the lawyer actually performing the service. Criticism of fee splitting and referral fee practices have caused all states to prohibit such practices unless certain conditions are met. While these conditions vary from state to state, they generally provide that a lawyer may not divide a fee for legal services with another lawyer who is not a partner or in association in the same firm, unless: (1) the client consents to the employment of the second lawyer after the full disclosure of the fee division to be made, (2) the fee division is proportionate to the legal services performed and the responsibility assumed by each of the lawyers, and (3) the total legal fee paid by the client does not exceed what would have been paid if only one lawyer had been involved.

Unfortunately, some lawyers continue to engage in referral fee and fee-splitting practices which do not meet the above-described conditions or the law in the state in which the lawyer practices.

Before hiring a lawyer and signing a fee agreement, be sure you inquire as to whether that lawyer will personally be providing the service needed or merely intends to refer you to another lawyer and obtain a fee for doing so. If you are advised that the lawyer you contact intends to refer you to another lawyer, insist on answers to the following questions:

- Why am I being referred to another lawyer?
- How did you select the particular lawyer to whom you are referring me?
- Do you personally recommend this lawyer?
- What do you know about the lawyer to whom you are referring me?
- Is the lawyer to whom you are referring me a specialist in the field of law to which my problem relates?
- Will you get a fee for referring me to this other lawyer?
- If you will receive a fee, how much will it be?
- When will you receive your fee?
- Will you continue to be involved in my legal matter?
- If so, to what extent and who will be primarily responsible?

Some lawyers, because of their friendship with another lawyer, or a feeling of an obligation to a particular lawyer based on some prior referral from him, will recommend a lawyer without adequate consideration as to whether the lawyer being recommended is truly best suited (i.e., competent) to provide the needed legal service. Remember, the best way to protect yourself from being referred to the wrong lawyer is to make your own investigation and determination as to whether or not the lawyer to whom you are referred is in fact the right lawyer for you.

YOU DECIDE HOW
THE LAWYER WILL BILL YOU

Many of the complaints and criticisms about lawyers center on their failure to keep clients informed about what action is being taken to solve the client's problem. Frequently, the only regular communication between a lawyer and a client is the lawyer's bill for legal fees and costs. When little or no other information about the progress of the matter is being passed on to the client, this practice can cause the client to react with a sense of bewilderment if not anger. "When, if ever, is the legal problem going to be resolved?"

How a lawyer bills a client, the manner in which the billing statement is prepared, and the content of the billing statement vary greatly from lawyer to lawyer depending on such factors as the nature of the fee to be charged, whether or not the lawyer records his time, and how that time is recorded.

If the lawyer's billing statement is improperly prepared, it offers little information to a client other than the dollar amount due and payable to the lawyer. If properly prepared, a lawyer's billing statement offers an excellent opportunity for the client to periodically monitor the lawyer's activity. To illustrate this, consider a typical *and improper* billing statement format used by some lawyers:

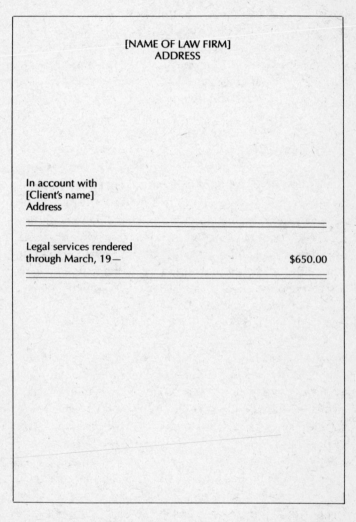

[NAME OF LAW FIRM]
ADDRESS

In account with
[Client's name]
Address

Legal services rendered
through March, 19—   **$650.00**

The only useful information in such a statement is the dollar amount due and payable to the lawyer and the month and year for which the charges were rendered. The client has no knowledge of what services were actually rendered, the date when the services were rendered, the time required to perform each service, or its cost. Neither is there any indication of what non-legal fee costs, if any, were incurred during the billing period. No wonder many clients, on receiving such billing statements, feel angry and frustrated.

Before considering the type of billing statement you should *insist* that your lawyer submit to you, let us consider for a moment the manner in which lawyers maintain a record of the time they expend in providing services to various clients. Some lawyers do not maintain a formal record of time but merely estimate the time expended on behalf of a particular client. Other lawyers maintain accurate and detailed records to reflect the date any service is rendered, the nature of that service, the time required to perform the service, and the dollar amount of fees incurred by the client by reason of such service. Obviously, a lawyer maintaining such a detailed record of time expended on behalf of a client is in a better position to bill a client based on actual services provided and time expended than is a lawyer who attempts to recall, on a monthly or other interval, services performed and the time required to perform such services.

DEMAND AN ITEMIZED BILLING

Now let us consider the kind of lawyer-billing format which you should *insist* upon receiving from the lawyer you hire. Remember, as the one paying for the legal service rendered, you have every right to demand that the lawyer you hire submit his billing statement to you in a format which you find acceptable. The following is an illustration of a suggested billing format which will provide you with the information you need if you are to monitor the lawyer's performance and to insure that you are receiving adequate legal representation and are paying only for those services actually rendered.

[NAME OF LAW FIRM]
ADDRESS

In account with   In Re [Legal Matter]
[Client's name]
Address

For professional services rendered through March 31, 19—
SERVICES RENDERED

3/2	JS	Conference with client; review of client documents and records; review of complaint served on client; preparation of letter to lawyer for opposing party	1.2 hrs. × $60 = $ 72.00
3/8	RW	Research re defenses available to client; preparation of memorandum re same	.9 hrs. × $40 = $ 36.00
3/8	JS	Preparation of client answer to complaint; preparation of notice of deposition of opposing party; preparation of request for production of documents of opposing party; telecon to client	1.4 hrs. × $60 = $ 84.00
3/21	JS	Conference with client; preparation for deposition of opposing party; take deposition of opposing party; review records of opposing party	2.1 hrs. × $60 = $126.00

TOTAL FEES: $318.00

COSTS AND DISBURSEMENTS

Clerk, Superior Court, filing
fee re Answer to Complaint $ 49.00

Judy Jones, Certified Shorthand
Reporter; Appearance fee and
transcript of deposition of
opposing party $115.00

TOTAL COSTS: $164.00

TOTAL FEES, COSTS & DISBURSEMENTS $482.00

1. **Account identity**. Specifying the particular account to which the billing statement relates is important if you have more than one matter being handled by the same lawyer or law office. You should receive separate statements for each account.

2. **End of billing period**. This feature establishes the last date of the billing statement.

3. **Activity date**. Reflects the date during the month of the billing period when each legal service was performed.

4. **Lawyer's initials**. Identifies the particular lawyer who performed each individual legal service.

5. **Service performed**. A brief but adequate description to keep you informed of the legal service performed.

6. **Time expended**. Reflects the amount of time necessary to perform the described legal service.

7. **Billing rate**. Sets forth the billing rate of the lawyer who performed the service. *

8. **Service cost**. Indicates the actual cost to you of each service performed by each lawyer on each date during the billing period. *

9. **Total fees**. Shows the total of all fees incurred for services rendered during the billing period. *

10. **Costs and disbursements itemization**. Identifies each cost and disbursement during the billing period.

11. **Total costs and disbursements**. Shows the total of all costs and disbursements incurred for services rendered during the billing period.

12. **Total fees, costs, and disbursements**. Shows total amount of legal fees,* costs, and disbursements incurred during billing period.

*Would not be shown if lawyer providing legal services on contingent fee basis.

As is apparent, the sample itemized billing statement shown provides a wealth of information with which to determine both what your lawyer is doing and whether the legal fees he is submitting to you are justified.

At this point you may be thinking, "Sure, I can tell the lawyer I hire how I want my bill submitted, but what do I do if the lawyer refuses?" The simple answer is that you *do not pay him!*

Many lawyers have business clients who think nothing of dictating to the lawyer the format by which the lawyer is to submit his billing statements. If the lawyer wants the client's business, he agrees to do so. You, as an individual client, have the same right to insist the lawyer you hire submit an itemized billing statement in a format acceptable to you. If the lawyer does not wish to do so, don't hire him. There is nothing unreasonable about your requesting that the lawyer you hire account for his time expended on your behalf and that he do so in a manner which is both acceptable and understandable to you. After all, you're the one paying for that time and have a right to expect nothing less than a full accounting.

The fact that a lawyer accepts a case on a contingent fee basis, where no legal fees are to be incurred unless the lawyer is successful in the pursuit of the client's claim, should make no difference in the client's right to receive, on request, an itemized monthly statement showing all of the information set forth above, with the important exception that no dollar amount will be due and payable by the client. Some lawyers hired on a contingent fee basis feel no obligation to maintain a record of the amount of time they expend pursuing a client's claim because they feel that unless the claim is successfully pursued, there will be no fee obligation. Consequently, they feel there is no need to maintain a record, or to forward to the client an itemization of his work. Such a lawyer is likely to conclude that if the claim is successfully pursued, his fee will be based on the amount of the recovery, and not on the number of hours expended in that effort.

Unfortunately, not all lawyer/client relationships proceed smoothly and, on occasion, it is necessary for a lawyer to withdraw from a case, or for the client to discharge that lawyer for misconduct. When this occurs on a contingent fee case, there is often an issue as to what, if anything, the lawyer is entitled to receive for his work to the date of withdrawal or discharge. If the lawyer has not maintained an ongoing record, the amount of his claim for legal fees is difficult, if not impossible, to verify. To protect yourself as a client, you should insist, even if you hire a lawyer on a contingent fee basis, that he maintain an accurate record of his time and activity on your behalf. By receiving and reviewing the lawyer's itemized monthly statement showing his time and activity on your behalf, you can keep informed in this regard and know whether the lawyer you hired, on a contingent fee basis or otherwise, is vigorously pursuing your legal claim.

THE FEE AGREEMENT: INSIST THAT IT BE IN WRITING

After negotiating an acceptable fee arrangement with the lawyer you intend to hire, it is important that you insist that the fee arrangement be put in writing. In this manner, both you and the lawyer will know exactly what is expected of each other with respect to legal fees.

62   In addition to having it in writing, the fee agreement should clearly set forth the circumstances upon which you must pay legal fees, the manner in which those fees will be computed, and the manner in which payment is to be made. If the lawyer is hired on an hourly basis, the dollar amount per hour for services to be rendered should be specified. If the lawyer is hired on a contingent fee basis, the manner in which the contingent fee is to be determined should also be written out. The absence of a written fee agreement clearly expressing the intention of the parties is a frequent cause of trouble in the lawyer/client relationship.

"The minute you read something and you can't understand it, you can almost be sure it was drawn up by a lawyer. Then, if you give it to another lawyer to read and he don't know just what it means, why then you can be sure it was drawn up by a lawyer."

Will Rogers

Typically, it is the lawyer who will prepare the fee agreement and submit it to you for signature. If, on reading the agreement, it is not clear, or does not contain all of the provisions you wish included, such as reference to the law-

yer's willingness to submit itemized monthly billing statements to you, insist the agreement be redrafted so that it is
clear to you and contains those provisions you wish included. *Do not sign the agreement until this has been done.*
Finally, be sure you obtain a copy of the agreement showing the lawyer's signature and keep it in a safe place.

CAUTION:
BEWARE OF INHERENT CONFLICTS

A lawyer's privilege to practice law carries with it the highest duty which the law can impose upon one person acting
for another. As a lawyer's client, you are entitled to have
your lawyer act with the highest degree of trust and fairness
in dealing with you. But lawyers, like others, have material
needs for themselves and their families, and are dependent
on legal fees to meet those needs. It is this very need to
receive legal fees that creates an inherent conflict in a lawyer's dealings with his own client.

In theory, a lawyer must set aside his own interest in favor of
the best interest of his client. When this is considered in the
context of a written fee agreement, usually drafted by the
lawyer, it becomes readily apparent that the lawyer's first
duty is to prepare one which is in the best interest of his
client. But some lawyers, when drafting such an agreement,
include provisions which are intended to protect themselves first, and the client thereafter.

No doubt most lawyers act fairly in discussing fee arrangements with prospective clients and in the preparation of
written fee agreements. But the danger does exist in such
situations that a lawyer will find it difficult not to include
provisions for his own protection, even though those provisions are not in the best interest of the client. Until the legal

profession or the state legislatures see fit to require all legal fee agreements to be reviewed and approved by an independent third party, before the client becomes obligated by such an agreement, the present practice by which fee agreements are entered into will no doubt continue.

If you are concerned over the fairness of a proposed fee agreement, ask the lawyer to fully explain the agreement to you and then confer with a trusted friend, business associate, or advisor before signing the agreement. You should not hesitate to consider a proposed fee agreement for a few days before deciding whether you wish to sign the agreement. It should go without saying that you should not sign that agreement unless you fully understand each and every provision.

FEE OBLIGATION ON WITHDRAWAL OR DISCHARGE OF THE LAWYER

On occasion, a lawyer will withdraw from representing a client before completing the service for which he was hired. His withdrawal might be due to an incapacitating mental or physical condition, or it may stem from some action of the client, such as pursuing an illegal course of conduct, or initiating a lawsuit solely for the purpose of harassing or maliciously injuring another person. When such a withdrawal occurs, the question invariably arises as to what fee obligation, if any, the client owes the lawyer.

Generally, a client's fee obligation to a withdrawing lawyer will depend on the reason for the withdrawal. If the client's conduct was the cause of the withdrawal, the client may have an obligation to pay the withdrawing lawyer in full, according to the terms of the fee agreement, or at least up to the point of his withdrawal.

If you discharge the lawyer for cause (i.e., because of the lawyer's misconduct), it is likely you will have no fee obligation to that lawyer. However, if the discharge is without cause and merely because you wish to change lawyers or for some other reason, you may well have an obligation to pay the lawyer for his work to the date of discharge. Here again, we see the importance of an itemized monthly billing statement in determing the amount of your fee obligation to him, be it hourly or contingent. If, however, your lawyer initiates the withdrawal, your fee obligation obligation to him will most likely depend on the lawyer's reason for withdrawing. If, for example, the lawyer is obligated by law to withdraw, based on some conduct on your part which requires it, you may well have an obligation to pay him the reasonable value of his services to the date of withdrawal. But, if the lawyer withdraws for some other reason unrelated to anything you did or did not do, any fee obligation will depend on the particular circumstances of that withdrawal.

EXCESSIVE LEGAL FEES: WHAT YOU CAN AND SHOULD DO ABOUT THEM

Excessive legal fees are probably the single greatest complaint made against lawyers by their clients. Fees are also a cause of great anxiety and concern when contemplating the hiring of a lawyer. However, knowing the factors that go into the formulation of legal fees, both from your lawyer's as well as your own point of view, how to interpret them, and what action to take when you believe you are being unjustly charged can save you many hours of worry and many dollars as well.

"When the lawyers are through what is there left, Bob? Can a mouse nibble at it and find enough to fasten a tooth in?"

Carl Sandburg

According to the legal profession, a lawyer's fee is considered excessive when a lawyer of "ordinary prudence" (whatever that is) has reviewed the facts and is left with a firm conviction that the fee is excessive. If you are the lawyer whose fee is being reviewed by another lawyer, such a definition of what constitutes an excessive legal fee may well be acceptable. But as a client, it is hardly comforting to think of one lawyer reviewing the facts surrounding another lawyer's legal fee in order to decide whether or not that charge is excessive.

From your standpoint as a client or prospective client, you should consider a legal fee excessive whenever it appears to be unjustifiable, based on the service you have received. Admittedly, this is a subjective test. But no apology need be made since you are the one being asked to pay. As such, you have the right not only to question the manner in which each of the services was provided by the lawyer, but also to question the charge for each of them.

Unfortunately, far too many clients who feel their lawyers' fees are excessive will complain privately when faced with an apparently excessive legal fee and then pay it anyhow!

By doing so, without calling the lawyer's attention to their true feelings, clients thus begin to harbor feelings of resentment or mistrust toward the lawyer, a development that invariably damages the relationship.

There is nothing taboo about discussing a fee which you feel is excessive with your lawyer. In fact, a prompt discussion after the charges have been received is nearly always healthy to the relationship. It is only an extremely callous lawyer who will disregard a client's concern about a legal fee once it has been brought to his attention. Admittedly, there are no hard and fast rules on what you should do when faced with an excessive legal fee, other than to bring it promptly to the attention of your lawyer. However, the following is a suggested guideline for challenging a fee presented to you by your lawyer.

Step No. 1:

Carefully review the lawyer's billing statement in question. Write down each charge that you feel is excessive and why you feel that it is.

Step No. 2:

Telephone your lawyer and request a meeting to discuss his billing statement. Insist on a face-to-face meeting with the lawyer and do not settle for a telephone discussion of the matter. Although more difficult than a telephone discussion, a face-to-face meeting is important if you are to fully air the matter, and if the lawyer is to become impressed with the extent of your concern and your desire to obtain his explanation.

Step No. 3:

Meet with your lawyer and have a full discussion of your feelings concerning the billing statement, the individual charges on the billing statement which you feel are excessive, and any other matter pertaining to it.

Step No. 4:

If your lawyer concurs in your belief that the fee is excessive, and is willing to reduce it, request that the billing statement be resubmitted to you showing the reduced fee. In this way, you will have a record of the corrected statement. If you are unable to reach agreement with your lawyer after a full discussion of the matter, thank him for his time and tell him you wish to consider the matter further before deciding what action to take. Indicate you will contact him again in a few days.

Step No. 5:

Confer with a trusted friend, business associate, or other advisor about the matter. Explain the lawyer's position, as well as your own, and ask for an opinion as to whether the fee charge in issue seems justified.

Step No. 6:

After considering the advice of your friend, business associate, or advisor, and your own feelings, as well as the explanations of your lawyer, decide whether you wish to pay the disputed fee. If you do not, immediately search for another lawyer who can be hired to replace your original lawyer in providing or completing the legal service you need. Confer with your new lawyer on the matter of how to

resolve the disputed fee matter involving your original
lawyer.

Remember, to supress your feeling of having been exces-
sively charged will invariably affect your relationship with
your lawyer adversely.

Many local and state bar associations have established procedures for the resolution of lawyer/client disputes regarding legal fees. Most procedures are voluntary, and vary in
method of operation, but usually provide for both the lawyer and the client to submit the matter to arbitration. At
least one state (California) has made it mandatory that the
lawyer submit to arbitration *any* dispute concerning legal
fees where such arbitration is requested by the client. Consult your telephone directory for the local bar association in
your community or see Appendix B for the address and
telephone number of the state bar association in your state.
By contacting the local or state bar association where you
reside, you can determine what procedures to follow and
what assistance may be provided in resolving a dispute
between you and your lawyer regarding legal fees. Also,
you can write to the American Bar Association Community
Dispute Services Department at 1155 East 60th Street,
Chicago, Illinois, 60637, (312) 947-4000, for information
on how you can receive assistance in resolving a dispute
with your lawyer over legal fees.

PROHIBITIVE LEGAL FEES:
SOME AVAILABLE ALTERNATIVES

As distinguished from excessive legal fees, prohibitive fees
(and sometimes related costs as well) are those which are
considered by the client to be fair but which the client
simply cannot afford to pay. Typically, this situation arises

when the client is receiving legal services on the basis of an hourly fee arrangement and engaged in a lengthy lawsuit. Then, because of some unexpected occurrence, such as a family emergency, the loss of employment, or other financial hardship which was not foreseen, the client simply cannot afford to continue paying for the legal services for which the lawyer was hired. When this occurs, what can be done?

To begin with, the client should immediately advise his lawyer of the problem and request a meeting. At such a meeting, the client and his lawyer should discuss the alternatives available. These include: (1) a temporary suspension of the lawyer's activities on behalf of the client; (2) renegotiating the fee arrangement between lawyer and client; (3) considering the employment of another lawyer whose fees are less; (4) reducing the scope of the lawyer's activity on behalf of the client; and (5) the initiation of settlement discussions if the client is pursuing a claim.

Each of these alternatives creates substantial risk to the client. If the lawyer temporarily suspends his activity on the client's behalf, the client's cause may well be prejudiced. And convincing a lawyer to renegotiate a fee arrangement may not be easy. Even if the lawyer agrees, the client is in a weak bargaining position. The hiring of another lawyer in the middle of a lawsuit or other legal matter is full of danger and may prove more costly than staying with the existing lawyer. Requesting the lawyer to reduce his activity on the client's behalf will increase the risk that the client receives less than adequate legal service. And lastly, initiating settlement negotiations on a client's claim solely because the client can no longer afford the legal services necessary to pursue the claim may well result in an unfavorable settlement.

Still, one or more of the alternatives discussed above—and the attendant risks—may have to be selected. It is a sad but true fact that both the quality and quantity of legal services a client receives is directly related to the client's ability to pay for such services. On occasion, a client simply cannot afford to pay for the "justice" to which he or she might otherwise be entitled.

> ## "Unless the legal profession ensures that no one in this country shall be denied legal assistance because of lack of resources, the government will make us do it...."
>
> **Thomas Ehrlich**
> **Former President, Legal Services Corporation**

SOME ALTERNATIVES TO LEGAL FEES

Provided you qualify, there are alternatives to the paying of legal fees for obtaining needed legal services. Among these alternatives are the following:

Legal Aid Services

These services, known as legal aid offices, legal aid societies, and legal service organizations, exist in hundreds of locations throughout the United States. Generally speaking, these services, funded by federal and state government, local and national bar associations, as well as special grants and private contributions, provide legal services to the poor in such areas as consumer needs, education, employment discrimination, food stamp programs, housing matters, juvenile rights, health matters, landlord/tenant disputes, small business licensing, senior citizen matters, social security, and welfare. Some services even draft simple wills and contracts, and provide assistance with adoptions, guardianships, and the collection of small debts.

Because these services were developed to deal primarily with problems of the poor, and for the most part operate on limited budgets, many of the service offices are short staffed and lacking the funds to handle more than the most simple or routine legal problems of the poor.

Although no national telephone directory listings for such service offices exists, you are likely to find the listing for the legal aid service office nearest you under one of the following headings: Legal Assistance, Legal Aid Office, Legal Aid Society, Community Legal Service, or some similar reference beginning with the name of the city or county in which you reside. If you experience difficulty in locating such an office, contact the local bar association in your community or the state bar association in your state for assistance. Appendix B contains a listing of the address and telephone number of state bar associations throughout the United States.

For additional information on the availability of legal aid services, write to the National Legal Aid and Defenders Association (NLADA), Suite 602, 21 M Street, N.W., Washington, D.C., 20037, for a copy of The Directory of

Legal Aid and Defender Services ($6.00) or write to the Legal Services Corporation, 500 N. Michigan Avenue, Chicago, Illinois, 60611.

Prepaid Legal
Service Plans

Such plans, developed in response to high legal fees and costs charged by lawyers, and the difficulty many people experience in finding a competent lawyer to provide a needed legal service, have become increasingly attractive to labor unions, cooperatives, and consumer organizations as a means of providing members in the lower or middle income range with needed legal services which might otherwise be inaccessible. It has been estimated that more than 150 prepaid legal service plans are now operating in the United States, affecting more than 2,000,000 individuals, and several million people may be members of such plans within a few years.

Typically, these plans offer legal services to plan members in subject areas such as will drafting, divorce, marital separation agreements, support and custody matters, adoptions, real estate transactions, landlord/tenant disputes, bankruptcy, personal injury claims, employment claims, income tax returns, and criminal proceedings.

Varying greatly in their method of operation and the particular services offered, such plans generally provide specified legal services in exchange for a prepayment by the plan member. In some cases, an employer makes the payment as a negotiated fringe benefit.

74

If you are considering membership in such a plan, it is suggested that you ask the following questions before becoming a member:

- How long has the plan been operating?
- How is the plan administered?
- How many members does the plan have?
- What legal services are offered by the plan?

It is important that you carefully review the scope of the services offered by the plan of which you are a member or are considering joining. Try to determine what your present and future legal needs will be and check to insure that the plan offers those services.

- How are lawyers selected to provide plan members with offered legal services?
- How many lawyers are available to provide offered services?
- Will I be restricted to a particular lawyer in obtaining the offered services?

Some plans designate a particular lawyer or group of lawyers whom its members must utilize, while other plans permit members to use lawyers of their own selection or who are on an approved list. If you will be restricted to the use of a particular lawyer, you may wish to meet with that lawyer before deciding whether to become a member of the plan.

- How do I get in touch with a lawyer to obtain an offered service?
- Will I receive an annual financial statement showing the income and expenses of the plan if I become a member?

■ Is there a grievance procedure to resolve disputes between plan members and lawyers?

For information on these plans, their availability in the
community where you live, and how you can start such a
plan, write or call The Resource Center for Consumers of
Legal Services, a non-profit organization established to
analyze, produce, and promote effective techniques for developing such plans, at 1302 18th Street, N.W.,
Washington, D.C., 20036, (202) 569-8514.

Prepaid Legal
Expense Insurance

Available to individuals or small businesses in nearly all
states, such insurance generally provides the insured with
protection against legal fees and costs to a specified
maximum limit in exchange for a premium charge. Typically, such insurance pays for consultation by the insured
(client) with a lawyer as well as defense and court costs, but
does not provide coverage for judgments rendered against
the insured. Specific coverage varies from policy to policy,
depending on the company offering the insurance, as well
as the premium which the insured is willing to pay.

For information on the availability of such insurance and
whether or not you qualify, contact your local insurance
broker, or write to NAS Insurance Services, Inc., P.O. Box
54831, Los Angeles, California, 94054, (213) 451-4988, or
Midwest Mutual Insurance Company, 1501 42nd Street,
West Des Moines, Iowa, 50265, (515) 223-2000, for the
office nearest you.

Public Interest
Law Services

The phrase "Public Interest Law," while having no generally accepted definition, is used to describe those legal
services offered to individuals and groups having legal
problems which are considered matters of public interest as
well.

Most public interest law services relate to matters involving
the environment, land use, racial discrimination, voting
rights, employment discrimination, consumer protection,
civil rights, mental health, civil liberties, education, and
constitutional rights. Although such services do vary wide-
ly, the common denominator for providing them is the existence of a strong public interest issue affecting many
people.

In recent years, lawyers interested in providing such services have formed public interest law firms, many of which
are affiliated with existing organizations. These law firms
and organizations are generally supported by charitable
foundations, membership subscriptions, or court-awarded
legal fees and costs.

Most public interest law services are offered through organizations and firms existing in California, New York, and
Washington D.C., but some services are available in other
parts of the United States, particularly in the more urban
areas. See Appendix C which contains a partial list of such
organizations and firms including addresses and telephone
numbers.

3 The Important First Meeting: How You Should Prepare

In considering whether or not to hire a particular lawyer, your first meeting with him is likely to be the most important. Your thorough preparation, the ability to clearly explain your legal problems, knowing what questions to ask the lawyer, and being able to evaluate the lawyer's answers to those questions will determine whether you obtain the legal service you need or merely add to your existing problem.

If you have never hired a lawyer, you may approach the meeting with a feeling of apprehension or anxiety. The stress of your legal problem, uncertainty as to the legal fees you will incur, or feelings of intimidation and rejection by the lawyer may combine with a natural reluctance to admit and discuss your problem with a stranger. If you have experienced dissatisfaction with a previous lawyer, however, you may approach such a meeting with a preconceived, but nevertheless incorrect belief that you have now learned your lesson and know exactly how to deal with your new lawyer.

To obtain the maximum benefits that a first meeting can offer, it is important and necessary that you overcome your apprehension, uncertainty, or fear, and discard any preconceived ideas you may have about how to hire a lawyer.

Such a meeting, if properly conducted by *you*, will provide you with a wealth of information with which to make an *informed* decision on whether or not you wish to hire the lawyer with whom you are meeting. Without doubt, the lack of proper preparation for such a meeting, and the failure to adequately evaluate the lawyer before he is hired, are causes of much client dissatisfaction.

Many so-called "sophisticated" clients, those who have frequent occasion to hire and use lawyers because of the client's business dealings, know that there is no substitute for proper evaluation of a lawyer before deciding whether that lawyer should be hired. Consider, for example, how insurance companies go about hiring lawyers to represent their insured. Such companies usually require the lawyer under consideration to submit written resumes detailing their background, professional education, and experience. References are also required and checked. A lawyer's "track record" in trial work is also examined. If the lawyer appears qualified, he is placed on the insurance company's "approved" list. Thereafter, he handles lawsuits in which the insurance company is obligated, by the terms of its policy, to provide a defense for an insured client.

This same procedure can be used by you when you need to hire a lawyer. Let us now discuss the process by which you can determine whether a particular lawyer is qualified and should therefore be place on *your* approved list.

TELEPHONING THE LAWYER'S OFFICE TO SCHEDULE THE MEETING

The first step in your search for the right lawyer is to obtain the names and phone numbers of at least three lawyers whom you wish to consider. Why three? Just as good consumer behavior dictates comparison shopping in purchasing any service or product, so too should comparison shopping be used when finding and hiring a lawyer. Only by conferring with a number of lawyers can you develop the information and insight necessary to determine which, among the various lawyers you consult, is best for you.

Consulting your list, telephone the office of each of the lawyers and, if the lawyer is available, describe the purpose of your call, the general nature of your problem, and be sure to ask each of the following questions:

- Is my problem the type you commonly handle?

It is important that you find out immediately whether the lawyer you are contacting is familiar with the area of law to which your problem relates and if he provides the legal service you need. If you learn he does not, or does so only infrequently, you should not hire him.

- When can we meet to discuss my problem?

The willingness of a lawyer to meet with you promptly will provide some indication as to whether he will act with equal promptness in handling your legal needs. If your problem is urgent, or causing you anxiety, and you want it solved as soon as possible, you will want a lawyer who will understand your legal problem, sympathize with your concern, and act accordingly.

- Will there be a cost for the first meeting and, if so, what will it be?

Many lawyers do not charge for the first meeting with a prospective client. Still, you are entitled to know and should know in advance whether the lawyer with whom you intend to meet will charge you for that meeting. You can then decide whether or not to meet with him.

- What is your standard fee or fee arrangement in handling problems such as mine?

Getting a lawyer to commit himself to a "ballpark" fee figure before you actually meet with him will give you needed time in which to consider how to ask about possible fee arrangements in light of your own financial condition and the lawyer's estimate. Do not decide against meeting with one of the lawyers merely because he has quoted a higher fee than others. It may be that the lawyer who has quoted the higher fee is better qualified and will be able to perform the services in less time, in a more professional manner, and with a net savings to you.

- If you become my lawyer, will you confirm the employment and fee arrangement in writing?

If the lawyer answers "no" to this question, or avoids a "yes" answer, you should save yourself the trouble of meeting with him. Any lawyer unwilling to commit himself in writing to an employment and fee arrangement is not a lawyer you should hire.

- How should I prepare for our meeting?
- What should I bring with me?

How the lawyer answers these questions will give you a good indication of his familiarity with problems of the type you are facing. It will also provide some indication as to the thoroughness with which he intends to conduct the meeting. The more thorough the first meeting, the more informed you will be when making a decision of whom to hire. A competent lawyer will not provide legal advice over the telephone to a stranger. Instead, he will ask some key questions in order to get an idea of what the prospective client's problem is, and he will usually request that all written materials pertaining to that problem be brought to the first meeting.

It is important during the telephone conversation with each of your prospective lawyers, or at least immediately afterward, to write down the answers you receive to each of your questions. Although it is recommended that you meet with each of the lawyers you telephoned, you may feel, after a comparison of the answers you receive in the first two meetings, that further meetings are unnecessary. If you do cancel a meeting, however, extend the courtesy of notifying the lawyer's office of the cancellation. Not only is his time just as important as your own, but the courtesy will likely work to your advantage should you, for one reason or another, wish to meet with him later.

PREPARING FOR
THE FIRST MEETING

By now you should be aware that finding and hiring the right lawyer requires careful preparation. There are no safe short-cuts to obtaining the information needed to make the best possible decision on whether or not to hire someone who could have a substantial influence on your affairs.

If you are thinking of taking an easy way out, such as relying on a friend's recommendation, or an advertisement, consider for a moment the typical frustration and anger you've heard about when someone has hired the wrong lawyer. In such a situation, the client must choose between staying with or discharging the lawyer. If the lawyer is discharged, another lawyer usually must be selected to pick up the pieces. This is not only expensive, it is also time-consuming and usually detrimental to the client's position since the work performed by the discharged lawyer must first be reviewed, and, to the extent it is deficient, redone, *if the circumstances permit*. Invariably, this will mean more legal expenses for the unfortunate client, and no compensation for the emotional wear and tear brought on himself by not taking the right steps in hiring a lawyer in the first place.

Before turning to the specifics of preparing for that first meeting, let us consider this whole thing from the lawyer's standpoint. Most likely, the lawyer in question will view your meeting as an opportunity to obtain new business, and this translates into legal fees. He may know the general nature of your case from the telephone conversation, but is probably unfamiliar with you or the details of your problem. He will know that if you have prepared thoroughly for the meeting, he will be able to more quickly understand your problem, determine whether or not he can provide the needed legal service, respond specifically to your various questions, and be able to determine what action should be taken immediately.

It is impossible to overemphasize the importance of adequate preparation *before* meeting with any prospective lawyer. So, you ask, "What do I do?"

Define Your
Legal Need

Begin your preparation by writing down a clear and concise statement of what you perceive your legal need or problem to be. From this will stem all other preparation for your meeting.

Accumulate All Writings
and Documents

All written material such as letters, documents, receipts, contracts, deeds, medical bills, repair estimates, cancelled checks, photographs, and anything else that you know or believe may be related to your legal need or problem should be accumulated. Avoid the potentially disastrous mistake many clients make in unilaterally excluding one or more writings from their lawyer's consideration because it seems too sensitive, personal, or irrelevant. If they are, a good lawyer will tell you so, and a "silly" omission could make or break your case. Also, it is vital to make a copy of everything you submit to your lawyer and keep these copies in a safe place, preferably a safe deposit box, in the event the originals are lost or misplaced.

Prepare a Written Chronology
of Important Facts

After you have accumulated all of the written materials which relate to your legal need or problem, put those writings in chronological order. Then, using such writings and your own recollection of the events leading up to your legal need or problem, write out in chronological order all of the important facts, dates, meetings, or other events which relate to your need or problem on a separate sheet.

Include the names, addresses, telephone numbers, and other pertinent information about each person who you believe has some connection with your problem, who may be a party or witness to the dispute, or for some other reason has information you believe may bear on your situation. The lawyer may wish to know about them, and he may wish to make further inquiry. Such a written chronology also provides you with an excellent reference for discussion during your meeting with the lawyer.

"Deceive not thy physician, confessor nor lawyer."

Proverb

Define the Legal Service You Desire

You may not know the exact legal service you need, but you should have a fairly good idea of what resolution you would like to achieve with the lawyer's help. Formulate a clear statement of what you believe the needed legal service is and how it can provide you with a solution to your problem. Also consider alternative solutions available. It may be that your first choice of a solution to your problem is not available because of some legal or other consideration. By writing down alternative solutions, you will be sure to discuss these alternatives during the first meeting with the lawyer and he can find out your preference among these solutions.

Prepare a List of Questions

The lawyer with whom you meet will surely ask you questions, and the information with which you respond will greatly assist the lawyer in understanding your problems and needs, and what action should be taken. Your responses will also give the lawyer an idea of what fee arrangement he should propose, and what he can expect from you as a client.

If the meeting is to be truly productive, it is important that you, and not just the lawyer, obtain the needed information with which to make an *informed decision* on whether to go forward with the lawyer/client relationship. Just as the lawyer will obtain the information he needs by asking questions, you must also ask questions and insist that the lawyer answer those questions honestly and unambiguously.

Often, it is not an easy task to sit in the office of a lawyer with whom you are unfamiliar and ask him numerous questions which will require the lawyer to engage in a frank discussion of his background, education, professional qualifications, and experience, all of which must be carefully examined if you are to make an informed decision about hiring him. To assist you in performing this task, it is suggested that you take time, before the meeting, to write down all the questions you will want to ask the lawyer. In this manner, you will have sufficient time to consider what you wish to ask and not overlook one or more important questions to which you should obtain answers.

The following is a suggested list of questions for your consideration in preparing your own list. The suggested list is by no means intended to be all-inclusive and you should not hesitate to add additional questions to your own list.

THE LAWYER'S BACKGROUND

- Where were you born?
- How old are you?
- Where do you reside?
- How long have you resided in the community?
- Are you married?
- How long have you been married?
- Do you have children?

Considered separately, it may seem unnecessary to ask a lawyer these questions. But the answers to these questions, considered collectively, will provide you with a fair profile of the lawyer's background. This is an important area of your inquiry since the relationship between you and your lawyer will be a close and confidential one in which you may be discussing such personal matters as those involving your family, employment, financial condition, estate planning, and will.

In considering your legal needs, both now and in the future, the lawyer's age may well be a factor. An elderly lawyer may not be your best selection if you are starting a new business or are involved in some dispute likely to result in a lengthy lawsuit. In such cases, a lawyer's advanced years may create an unnecessary risk that you will be required to replace him as your business continues to grow or before completion of the lawsuit. Conversely, a young lawyer may not have the experience of an older lawyer and therefore be unable to provide a needed legal service in as competent a manner. Also, some lawyers do not enter the field of law until their middle years, and, despite outward appearances of having practiced for many years, are relatively inexperienced as lawyers.

The length of time a lawyer has resided in a community, his marital status, and whether or not he is a parent all provide some basis for determining the lawyer's stability when considered in light of your own assessment of the importance of these factors.

THE LAWYER'S EDUCATION

- Where did you receive your college education?
- When did you graduate from college?
- What degree did you receive on graduation?
- Where did you receive your law school education?
- When did you graduate from law school?
- What degree did you receive on graduation?
- Do you hold any special degrees or certificates?
- Have you taken advanced courses to further your education?

If you are like some clients, you will be concerned about where the lawyer with whom you are meeting attended college and law school. Some clients believe one college provides a better education than does another and may feel more secure with a lawyer who attended a particular college. Likewise, with respect to law schools, some are considered better than others. Many years ago the American Bar Association established a procedure for the accreditation of law schools, and some clients prefer lawyers who have attended law schools so accredited.

An indication by the lawyer that he is continuing his formal legal education is an excellent sign that the lawyer is conscientious in his efforts to provide clients with competent service by keeping abreast of current developments in the law of the field in which he practices.

Finally, a lawyer's educational background may be extremely important, depending on the nature of your legal need. Consider, for example, the probable benefits of hiring a lawyer whose undergraduate education was in an engineering field if your legal need relates to a patent problem.

THE LAWYER'S
PROFESSIONAL QUALIFICATIONS

- What was your class standing in law school?
- When did you pass the State Bar Examination?
- Did you do so on your first attempt?
- How long have you been active in the practice of law?

There is usually a correlation between a lawyer's class standing in law school and his successful completion of the State Bar Examination on the first try. High class standing in law school is usually a good indication the lawyer was diligent in his study of law and has a good knowledge of the law. Both of these factors are fundamental to a lawyer's professional qualifications. When considered in the context of how long the lawyer has been practicing law, you should have a fairly good general indication of the lawyer's experience.

- Are you licensed to practice law in any other states?
- Do you have any special qualifications or certification as a lawyer?

Depending on the nature of your problem and the legal service you need, you may wish to hire a lawyer who is qualified to appear in court or otherwise practice law in another state. Normally, a lawyer licensed to practice in one state cannot practice law in another state unless he has been qualified there. However, there is a procedure which allows a lawyer not admitted to practice before a particular court the privilege of participating in a hearing or trial, if that court is satisfied that the lawyer is competent to do so, without requiring the lawyer to apply for formal admission.

- Do you have membership in any professional organizations?
- Are you active in any professional organizations?

A lawyer's membership in a professional organization can prove to be an advantage or disadvantage, depending on the nature of the organization, the lawyer's position in that organization, and the amount of time the lawyer expends in the pursuit of the organization's functions. Some lawyers, and their clients, have learned to their dismay that a lawyer's willingness to become an officer in a professional organization means the lawyer has little or no time available for his clients and the practice of law.

- Have you ever been disciplined by a state bar association?
- Is there presently a complaint pending against you with any state or local bar association?
- Have you ever been charged with criminal misconduct relating to your activities as a lawyer or otherwise?

You definitely want to know about prior disciplinary action taken against the lawyer. Your relationship with the lawyer you hire is too important not to know any adverse matter pertaining to the lawyer's background. This is especially true if the discipline relates to misconduct in the lawyer's manner of treating one of his clients, or the misappropriation of client monies for his own use. In some instances, a lawyer who has done so is temporarily suspended from the practice of law but is eventually reinstated. Whether or not you wish to hire such a lawyer, you should have the benefit of such information before you make that decision. In some instances, a lawyer has been accused of serious misconduct having a severely adverse impact on a client, but his hearing before the state bar association or other disciplinary body, which will determine whether or not to suspend or disbar him, has not yet begun. In such cases, you have a right to know of such a proceeding so that you can make an informed decision on whether or not to hire him.

■ Have you written a legal article for a professional journal or other publication?

If the lawyer has written a legal article, ask for a copy. By reading the material, you may learn more about the lawyer and the area in which he primarily practices law or exhibits special interest.

THE LAWYER'S PROFESSIONAL EXPERIENCE

■ What type of legal matters do you presently handle?
■ What type of legal matters have you handled in the past?
■ What type of experience have you had as a lawyer?
■ Have you handled problems similar to mine?
■ When did you last handle a problem similar to mine?
■ Do you still handle such problems?
■ What percentage of your total practice time as a lawyer is devoted to handling problems like mine?

There is a vast difference between a lawyer's technical qualifications to practice law and his actual experience with it—experience that gives his qualifications the benefit of sound judgment. You should not hesitate to ask the lawyer the questions suggested above.

You must know the history of the lawyer's practical experience in handling problems similar to yours if you are to make an informed decision on whether or not to hire him.

"... even the very best lawyers are usually truly competent and proficient in only a few areas of the law...."

Chesterfield Smith
Past President, American Bar Association

■ What percentage of the total time you practice law is spent on trial work?

Because of the nature of their practice, many lawyers never go to court. Most of the work such lawyers do is performed in their offices, and, if the need to appear in court on behalf of a client arises, the matter is referred to another lawyer competent in trial work. Other lawyers spend substantial time doing trial work, though this should not be construed to mean that they are in court most of the time. Many trial lawyers spend a good deal of their time doing what is termed "discovery." This is the preparation for trial, and involves such things as preparing pleadings, doing investigative work, taking depositions of parties and witnesses to lawsuits, and subpoenaing and reviewing records pertaining to issues raised by the lawsuit. Depending on the nature of your problem, you may or may not need a trial lawyer. It is becoming increasingly clear to both lawyers and non-lawyers that trial work is a specialty among lawyers.

Not all lawyers are suited for trial work, and some of those who claim to be trial lawyers are in fact only infrequently involved in performing such functions.

■ What work experience have you had other than as a lawyer which you believe helps you to practice law?

The prior work history of a lawyer may provide invaluable information in deciding which among two or more otherwise equally qualified lawyers should be hired. A lawyer with a background in real estate may well be better able to give you real estate law advice. Similarly, a lawyer with a background in construction may be better able to understand the technical jargon in a lawsuit involving structural or other defects in the construction of a building.

■ What are the names of present or former clients for whom you have provided legal services?
■ What are the names of former clients for whom you have provided legal services similar to those which I need?
■ What present or former clients can you identify as references?

The calibre of a lawyer's clients, or former clients, is usually a good indication of the lawyer's professional qualifications and experience. Successful businessmen, and others who have frequent need for the services of a lawyer, do not hire and continue to use a lawyer who is unable to perform the needed service, or does so only in mediocre fashion. By carefully examining a lawyer's clients, and the nature of the business in which those clients engage, you will have a fairly good indication of the type of law the lawyer practices. Many lawyers and law firms think nothing of listing a representative sample of their clients in directories in which they or their law firms are listed. As we discussed in Chapter One, the Martindale-Hubbell Law Directory contains a list of representative clients for many of the law firms listed. If for some reason the lawyer is reluctant to disclose the identity of his clients, you may obtain this information by asking others in the community where the lawyer practices.

EMPLOYMENT CONSIDERATIONS

- Do I need the professional assistance of a lawyer?

Some people who consult lawyers in the belief they need a legal service are actually in need of some other professional assistance such as that of a marriage counselor, a psychologist, a member of the clergy, or a social worker. You should not hesitate to carefully question the lawyer about the alternatives available to you in obtaining the assistance you need.

- What legal service do I need?
- Do I need the legal service immediately?

After a frank discussion, and before the first meeting ends, the lawyer should have a fairly good idea of what legal service you need. He should also know whether there is an urgency about providing that service and what action, if any, should be taken immediately. It is probably a bad sign if the lawyer seems uncertain as to what legal service you need, and whether the service is required immediately. Vagueness in responding to these questions may mean the lawyer does not have a working knowledge of the law related to your problem. No lawyer should be expected to know all of the law, and it is unrealistic to conduct your search for the right lawyer with the belief that he will know all of the law applicable to your problem without research or reflection.

- How do you anticipate solving my problems?
- What is the probable outcome of my legal matter?
- In what sequence will needed legal services be applied?

An experienced lawyer will have a reasonably accurate idea of how the legal problem you have will be solved through the application of a lawyer's efforts. But no lawyer can guarantee you a decision in your favor, and any lawyer who attempts to do so should be avoided. The steps or sequence by which legal services are applied to solving your problem will be known to an experienced lawyer and should be carefully explained so you will know what to expect.

- What is your best estimate as to the time it will take to provide the needed legal service and solve my problem?

An experienced lawyer should be able to provide you with a reasonably accurate estimate of the amount of time it will take to solve your legal problem. This will provide you with some information with which to make an estimate of the probable legal fees you will incur. However, you should consider the possibility of unforseeable circumstances changing the lawyer's estimate, and discuss this possibility with him.

- Will you personally perform the legal service I need?
- Are you involved in activities which will limit the time you have available for my legal needs?
- If someone other than yourself will perform all or part of the legal service I need, who is that person?
- When may I meet this other person?
- Who will supervise this other person in the legal service I need?

Many clients have learned to their dismay that some lawyer other than the one they hired performed most of the legal services they needed. Some firms consist of a number of lawyers, one or more of which may be excellent at getting business, but only marginally qualified at doing it. You should know in advance who will actually perform the legal service you need. Do not be misled by an experienced lawyer into believing that he will perform the needed service, and then find out that some inexperienced assistant has performed it. It is not uncommon for an experienced lawyer with an active practice to use assistants, but it should be understood clearly that those assistants are merely that— assistants—and not the primary lawyer responsible to you, the client, for providing the service which you have hired him to perform.

- Is there any matter which should be brought to my attention regarding a possible conflict of interest if I hire you as my lawyer?

We discuss in Chapter Four the matter of a conflict of interest in a lawyer's representation of one client whose interest is adverse to that of the lawyer, another of the lawyer's clients, or some third party. It is sufficient to say at this point that you should carefully question the lawyer as to a possi-

ble conflict of interest. Discovery of such a conflict later
may well necessitate searching for and hiring another
lawyer.

LEGAL FEE CONSIDERATIONS

- What is your usual fee arrangement for problems such as
mine?
- What is your standard hourly rate?
- What is the standard hourly rate for other lawyers in your
office?
- What percentage of the work you do as a lawyer is performed on an hourly fee basis?
- What percentage of the work you do as a lawyer is performed on a contingent fee basis?

If you read Chapter Two, you know that a full and frank
discussion of legal fees is imperative to a healthy lawyer/
client relationship. You should insist on such a discussion
and accept nothing less.

- What type of fee arrangement will you consider in this
matter?

Although you, the lawyer, or both may have a preliminary
idea of the type of fee arrangement you want, a discussion
of available alternative arrangements is to your advantage.
Try to consider each such alternative fee arrangement in
light of the other information you have obtained from the
lawyer. Also, the alternative fee arrangements indicated by
the other lawyers with whom you consult will provide an
excellent reference point for discussing and deciding what
fee arrangement you want.

- How will the legal fees I incur be determined?
- Will you or the other persons in your office who provide the legal services I need keep a record of the time you expend in providing those services?
- May I see an example of the method by which you and other persons in your office record their time on a client's matter?

If the legal services you need are extensive, and you are paying on an hourly basis, you will have correspondingly large legal fees. How a lawyer keeps his time may well mean the difference in hundreds, even thousands, of dollars in legal fees, and you should be satisfied that the method of recording such time is accurate and fair to you.

- What is your estimate of the total legal fees I am likely to incur?

An experienced lawyer should be able to provide you with a reasonably accurate estimate of the total legal fees you are likely to incur. But, as indicated above, unforeseeable circumstances may affect this estimate. Remember, you are only getting an estimate if the fee arrangement is on an hourly basis. If a contingent fee arrangement is agreed upon, the actual fee is, of course, dependent upon the amount recovered.

- What control will I have over the amount of legal fees I incur?
- What other costs am I likely to incur?
- Will I have control over the amount of these other costs?

The extent to which you exercise control over the amount of legal fees you will incur will depend on the degree to which you wish to become involved in the actual providing

of the needed legal services. You may wish to consider
requiring the lawyer you hire to notify you when the legal
fees reach a certain level. You may also require him to
notify you before incurring any costs or at least incurring a
cost over a specified dollar amount.

- What is your normal billing procedure?
- May I see an example of your standard billing statement?
- Do you provide clients with itemized monthly billing
statements if requested?
- Are you agreeable to providing me with monthly
itemized billing statements?

Again, we have discussed in Chapter Two the desirability of
receiving monthly itemized billing statements and there is
no need to repeat that information here. What is important
about these questions is that they will provide you with
needed information on whether the lawyer is agreeable to
your demand for such statements.

- As to non-lawyer personnel with your office who provide
some service in connection with your handling of my legal
matter, at what rate will I be billed for the services of those
individuals?

It is a good idea to find out who these non-lawyer personnel
are, what services they will perform in connection with
your legal matter, and the hourly rate or other basis upon
which you will be billed for those services. Unfortunately,
some lawyers utilize paralegals and others to perform many
office services for clients who are then billed at the lawyer's
rate, and not that of the paralegal or other non-lawyer person.

- Is my legal matter of the type which will entitle me to reimbursement for legal fees or costs?

Generally speaking, in the absence of an agreement between the parties to the contrary, the prevailing party in a lawsuit is not entitled to reimbursement from the losing party for legal fees incurred in pursuing the matter although some costs, such as filing charges, witness fees, and deposition costs may be recoverable. However, there are some federal and state statutes which provide for reimbursement of legal fees. This is an important matter about which you should carefully question the lawyer.

- What is the legal authority for such reimbursement?
- Who will decide the question of reimbursement?
- Will I get full or only partial reimbursement?

In some instances, a written agreement between parties who ultimately end up in a lawsuit will provide that the prevailing party in the lawsuit is entitled to "reasonable" legal fees and costs. What constitutes reasonable legal fees is normally a question of fact for the court to decide and it may not mean full reimbursement. Therefore, even if your legal matter is of such a nature as to entitle you to reimbursement for legal fees and costs, you must carefully question the lawyer as to the extent of such reimbursement.

- When will I know if I am entitled to reimbursement?
- Can my legal matter be handled in such a way as to entitle me to full reimbursement?

Depending on the nature of the legal matter, full reimbursement may be possible. Again, the lawyer should be questioned carefully as to his views on how your legal matter can be handled to insure the maximum possible reimbursement for your legal fees and costs.

THE LAWYER'S
OFFICE PROCEDURES

■ How will you maintain a record of the correspondence, pleadings, documents, and other writings pertaining to my legal matter?
■ What security do you have to insure the safekeeping of such written materials?

The manner in which lawyers maintain records pertaining to the legal matters of clients ranges from careful and complete records indexed for easy reference to a confusing mass of disorganized looseleaf papers tossed in one or more file folders through which the lawyer must thumb each time he needs to refer to a particular document. It is not uncommon for one lawyer to size up his opponent, in part, by how the opponent maintains his files and the degree to which the opponent appears organized in that regard. If you observe poorly maintained files on the lawyer's desk or on the floor around the lawyer's office, you have cause for concern that your file may receive similar treatment. You are entitled to have your file records properly maintained and placed in a file cabinet when not being used by the lawyer.

■ Will I have access on request to the file you maintain on my legal matter?

This topic is discussed in Chapter Four but it should be noted at this point that since you are the one paying for the lawyer's services, the records obtained or prepared by the lawyer are done so at your expense and on your behalf. As such, you have a right to request and insist on access to the file maintained by your lawyer.

- How will you preserve the confidentiality of communications between us?
- Who within your office will have access to the file you maintain on my legal matter?
- Will all members of your office staff be instructed not to discuss my legal matter with others?

Your right to confidentiality in the communications between yourself and your lawyer is also discussed in detail in Chapter Four. The degree to which you should express concern about the confidentiality of the communications between yourself and your lawyer depends in large part on the nature of your legal problem. Be aware that others within the lawyer's office, including non-lawyers, will likely have access to the file your lawyer maintains on your legal matter. If your legal matter is particularly sensitive, you should discuss the security and confidentiality of your communications with the lawyer in detail. Some law offices have a high turnover in secretarial and other staff positions and your legal matter may be viewed by more than one secretary working for the lawyer you hire. For this reason, as well as the possible lack of understanding on the part of the secretaries and others within the office as to the importance of preserving the confidentiality of communications between you and your lawyer, it is important your lawyer understand your desire that his office staff be periodically instructed in this regard.

- Do you have a calendar or diary system to insure that important dates pertaining to my legal problem will not be overlooked?

Many of the claims clients have, for which they seek the assistance of a lawyer, are affected by a limitation period during which the claim may be pursued. A lawyer's failure to file the claim within a specified time with a governmental agency or as a civil lawsuit may preclude the client's right to pursue the claim, even though it is otherwise perfectly valid. Many lawyers are sufficiently concerned about not overlooking an important date pertaining to a client's legal matter that they have not one but two calendar diary systems within their office. Frequently the lawyer and his secretary will maintain separate calendar or diary systems to insure that no important date is overlooked. Many applications submitted to lawyers who wish to obtain legal malpractice insurance require disclosure of the calendar or diary systems utilized by the lawyer. Insist that the lawyer you hire use such a system.

■ Do you maintain a duplicate recordkeeping system to protect against the accidental loss of a client's file?

It does not happen frequently, but from time to time a lawyer will misplace or lose a client's file. Lawyers often take such files with them to court, or to a meeting, and in the process it is carried in automobiles, on subways, in buses, and on airplanes. By having a duplicate file system within the office, the lawyer protects his client against the possibility of losing the client's file.

In addition to asking questions such as those suggested above, and insisting on clear answers from the lawyer with whom you are meeting, you should not hesitate to write down notes concerning the answers given by the lawyer. In order to accomplish this, you should take a notepad with you to the meeting. By making notes of the lawyer's answers, you will have a ready reference with which to evaluate the various lawyers with whom you meet. Also, if a dispute should develop with the lawyer you ultimately hire, you will have some record of the lawyer's representations to you at the outset of the relationship.

104   If you are married, and your legal matter is of such a nature as to permit, it is a good idea to take your spouse, or some other person with whom the matter can be openly and fully discussed, with you to the first meeting. Legal matters often affect both husband and wife, and the presence of your spouse will frequently assist you in selecting the right lawyer.

It is common for individuals in stressful situations to use "outside" support in meeting with lawyers, especially for the first time. Such support tends to relax the individual, help keep his or her mind clear, and give a valuable source of feedback after the meeting. Also, should you die or become incapacitated while the legal matter is being handled by the lawyer, the fact that your spouse or good friend met with the lawyer at the outset of the relationship will add to a sense of security about the continued handling of your legal matter.

While it may seem strange to imagine yourself sitting in a lawyer's office during a first meeting and asking numerous questions, the answers to which you are writing down or otherwise noting, no competent lawyer will take exception to your caution and thoroughness. In fact, it should impress the lawyer with your sincerity to have your legal matter handled in the best possible fashion. A competent lawyer will know you are merely attempting to make the lawyer/client relationship better for both of you.

THE EVALUATION AFTER
THE FIRST MEETING

If time and your legal needs permit, it is a good idea to wait a few days before attempting to evaluate the various lawyers with whom you have met. In this way, you will have time to consider carefully all of the information you have received from each of them. You will be able to compare your notes of their answers to your various questions, as well as what you observed by being in the offices of each of the lawyers (another reason for taking someone with you).

In conducting your evaluation, consider which lawyer appeared to have the most stable background, the best education, the best professional qualifications, and the most professional experience. Ask yourself which lawyer was most direct in answering your various questions; which was most open and frank in the discussion of legal fees, and which gave you the greatest sense of security and confidence. In the final analysis, your decision may very well come down to which lawyer you feel best about. The potential lawyer/client relationship, being a human one, reflects your feelings about the lawyer, and, if the lawyer is honest with himself, his own about you as a prospective client as well. It is imperative that the relationship begin with a proper feeling of trust and respect on both sides and with an understanding at the outset of what is expected by both of you.

A THANK-YOU NOTE

On deciding to hire one of the various lawyers with whom you met, remember to send the other lawyers a simple thank-you note. Although sometimes overlooked, it is an excellent way of expressing your appreciation for the time the lawyer took to meet with you, at your request, in your search for the lawyer you feel is right for you. Although the lawyer receiving such a thank-you note may not be your first choice, he may prove to be an excellent starting point if you suddenly find yourself in need of replacing the lawyer you did hire because of some unforeseen event such as the death or illness of the lawyer, a dispute with him, a conflict of interest, or some other reason.

CONFIRM THE EMPLOYMENT AND
FEE ARRANGEMENT IN WRITING

The importance of confirming the fee arrangement in writing has already been discussed in Chapter Two, and need not be belabored here. But it is not only the fee arrangement which should be in writing. The employment agreement with the lawyer should also be in writing to insure that both you and the lawyer you hire know exactly what is expected of each other. Too often a lawyer is hired on a vague oral understanding of what he is going to do on the client's behalf. If for some reason the relationship between the lawyer and the client deteriorates, there is no record to hold the lawyer to what the client recalls the understanding to have been. Many lawyer/client relationships have suffered severely from a memory loss, real or otherwise, and it is usually the client, not the lawyer, who suffers because of this. Reducing the employment arrangement to writing, which specifically indicates the purpose for which the lawyer is being hired, greatly reduces the chances of a misunderstanding, and you, as the client, have a record to protect you, should a dispute subsequently arise.

Such a written agreement is typically prepared by the lawyer and submitted to you for signature. When submitted, you should be sure the lawyer has already signed it and that you will receive a *signed* copy for your own file. If you do not fully understand each and every provision of the agreement, or it contains some provision inconsistent with what the lawyer previously indicated, ask him to explain the provision in question and then rewrite the agreement to clarify any objectionable matter. Only after this has been done, and you fully and clearly understand each and every provision of the agreement, should it be signed by you. Remember, the lawyer will probably hold you to the agreement and it should be sufficiently clear so there can be no misunderstanding as to what obligation the lawyer has to you by such an agreement.

Agreements relating to the employment of a lawyer and the fee arrangement between the lawyer and the client vary greatly from lawyer to lawyer and from community to community. The following examples are offered only for your consideration and to familiarize you with what a combined employment and fee agreement might contain. Any number of additional matters may need to be included in order to insure you the best protection and to define more precisely the duties of both the lawyer and the client. You should not hesitate to ask the lawyer to include any additional matter which you feel should be a part of the agreement so as to more clearly express in written form your desires relating to the legal services for which you are hiring the lawyer.

LAW OFFICES OF JONES AND SMITH
[Address]

[Date]

Mr. Robert Johnson
[Address]

RE: [Reference to legal matter]

Dear Mr. Johnson:

This letter will confirm my agreement to represent you in the above matter. Specifically, you have requested that I provide you with legal services [description of legal services to be rendered].

My services will be provided at the rate of $50 per hour plus costs. No costs will be incurred without your prior expressed approval and it is understood you will advance such sums as are necessary to pay costs.

You will receive monthly itemized billing statements showing the date of all services performed by me, a brief description of the service performed, the time required to perform the service, the legal fee for each service, an itemization of all costs incurred, and the total of all fees and costs for which you are billed.

Additionally, I will provide you with periodic status reports at least once every three months on the progress of your matter, and you will receive copies of all correspondence, pleadings, or other documents prepared by me as well as copies of all such writings relating to your matter which are received by me from others.

Please sign the enclosed copy of this letter to indicate your agreement and consent to the foregoing and return it to me in the envelope enclosed. You should retain this letter agreement.

Cordially,

JOHN JONES, ESQ.

JJ/ms

Agreed and consented to:

_____

MR. ROBERT JOHNSON

Hourly Fee Letter Agreement

LAW OFFICES OF JONES AND SMITH
[Address]

[Date]

Mr. Robert Johnson
[Address]

RE: [Reference to legal matter]

Dear Mr. Johnson:

You have consulted me with respect to [description of matter for which legal service is sought] and I have agreed to represent you with respect to this matter.

My fee for the services I will render will be a percentage of your net recovery (i.e., total amount of recovery less all costs which you have advanced) and shall be payable as follows: Twenty percent (20%) if your claim is settled without commencement of a lawsuit; twenty-five percent (25%) if a lawsuit is commenced and settlement occurs more than thirty days prior to the actual trial; thirty percent (30%) if settlement occurs within thirty days prior to the actual trial but before commencement of same; and thirty-three and one third percent (33⅓%) after commencement of trial. If an appeal is taken, I shall receive thirty-five percent (35%) of such net recovery to you, after final resolution of such appeal.

You will receive monthly itemized statements showing the date of any service performed by me, a brief description of the service performed, the time required to perform the service, and an itemization of all costs incurred. It is understood no costs shall be incurred without your prior approval and you will advance all sums necessary to pay costs.

I will provide you with periodic status reports at least once every three months on the progress of your matter, and you will receive copies of all correspondence, pleadings, or other documents prepared by me as well as copies of all such writings relating to your matter which are received by me from others.

Please sign the enclosed copy of this letter to indicate your agreement and consent to the foregoing and return it to me in the envelope enclosed. You should retain this letter agreement.

Cordially,

JOHN JONES, ESQ.

JJ/ms
Agreed and consented to:

_____

MR. ROBERT JOHNSON

Contingent Fee Letter Agreement

4 Your Rights as a Lawyer's Client

When you hire a lawyer you are reaffirming the existence of the near-exclusive right to practice law which lawyers have enjoyed for many years. When combined with the fact that lawyers are, for the most part, a self-regulated group, it becomes clear why lawyers have such influence in our communities and our government. For many years, the public was content to accept the argument so persuasively asserted by lawyers that only those possessed of special training (law school) and experience (the actual practice of law) should be engaged in so important a function as the practice of law in our society. But as ever-increasing emphasis has been placed on legal rights, and the public has become more sophisticated about legal matters and lawyers, it is becoming ever more obvious that the near-exclusive right to practice law which lawyers now enjoy can only be justified if: (1) lawyers are truly competent to provide needed legal services, (2) such services are available to all members of the public, and (3) such services are provided at a cost which all members of the public can afford. It is clear the public is no longer willing to accept the special status so long enjoyed by lawyers unless these conditions are met.

As with nearly all rights, the right to practice law carries with it certain obligations. It is these obligations which constitute your rights as a lawyer's client. If you are to become an informed consumer of legal services, you must know what your rights are.

Your Rights as a Lawyer's Client

In part, your rights as a lawyer's client have been acknowledged by the legal profession through the adoption by the American Bar Association of the Model Code of Professional Responsibility. This code has been adopted in some form in every state and is divided into three distinct but interrelated parts: Canons (statements of ethical responsibilities inherent in the practice of law and to which the conduct of all lawyers should conform), Ethical Considerations (aspirational statements to which all lawyers should strive in maintaining the highest standards of the legal profession), and Disciplinary Rules (statements of the minimum conduct below which lawyers will be subject to disciplinary action).

The Model Code of Professional Responsibility was drafted by lawyers, is intended for use by lawyers, and is not generally available to clients. In its entirety, it consists of many pages and even if every lawyer were required to provide a copy of the code to every client, it is unlikely that all clients would read the material. Therefore, what follows is a general discussion of what are felt to be among the most important of the various rights to which a client is entitled. Included in our discussion are the following: a competent lawyer who performs legal services in a competent fashion; confidentiality in all communications between the lawyer and the client; a full accounting of all client monies which the lawyer handles including fees, trust funds, settlement funds, and other property entrusted to the lawyer; a lawyer's undivided effort on behalf of a client; frank and full communication between lawyer and client; a client's participation in decision-making; properly maintained and accessible files; and the right to fire a lawyer at any time, with or without cause. We now turn to a discussion of each of these rights.

CANONS

Canon 1. A lawyer should assist in maintaining the integrity and competence of the legal profession.

Canon 2. A lawyer should assist the legal profession in fulfilling its duty to make legal counsel available.

Canon 3. A lawyer should assist in preventing the unauthorized practice of law.

Canon 4. A lawyer should preserve the confidences and secrets of a client.

Canon 5. A lawyer should exercise independent professional judgment on behalf of a client.

Canon 6. A lawyer should represent a client competently.

Canon 7. A lawyer should represent a client zealously within the bounds of the law.

Canon 8. A lawyer should assist in improving the legal system.

Canon 9. A lawyer should avoid even the appearance of professional impropriety.

Excerpted from Model Code of Professional Responsibility. As amended February, 1979, copyright American Bar Association.

COMPETENT PERFORMANCE

Criticism of lawyers and the legal profession is increasing at what lawyers can only consider an alarming rate. It comes from the President and Chief Justice of the United States as well as from the man in the street. Much of this criticism centers on the question of competence among various members of the legal profession. Some of this criticism is undoubtedly justified. Numerous studies have indicated a belief, both within and outside the legal profession, that some lawyers exhibit incompetence in their representation of clients.

You, as a lawyer's client, have an absolute right to professional competence from your lawyer both with respect to the lawyer's ability as well as the manner in which that ability is applied in providing you with the legal service for which you employed the lawyer. Being asked by a lawyer to pay his legal fee statement should only reaffirm your awareness of your right to truly competent performance.

At the very heart of the lawyer/client relationship is the expressed or implied representation by the lawyer that the client will receive the special competence necessary to provide the legal service which the client needs.

What, however, constitutes competence in a lawyer? Unfortunately, there is no generally accepted standard for determining competence in a lawyer. For most clients, the lawyer's competence is measured in terms of the client's satsifaction, the ability of the lawyer to anticipate and steer the client away from problems which could adversely affect the client, the promptness of the lawyer in delivering the needed legal service, the lawyer's research and writing abilities, and the lawyer's track record at resolving legal disputes both inside and outside the courtroom.

"...from one-third to one-half of the lawyers who appear in the serious cases are not really qualified to render fully adequate representation."

Warren E. Burger
Chief Justice, United States Supreme Court

No doubt, most lawyers would like their clients and prospective clients to believe that they have met all the high standards required for admission to the select group of those who have the right to practice law and hold themselves out in the community as lawyers. In truth, a lawyer need only meet certain minimum standards for admission in a state to practice law. Typically, a lawyer obtains a license to practice law after he has satisfied certain educational requirements and has successfully completed a state bar examination.

While there is a correlation between a lawyer's competence and his law school education, class standing, bar examination performance, on-the-job legal training, practical experience, association with fellow lawyers, and continuing legal education, it is clear that true competence is not obtained until these factors have had an opportunity to influence and supplement the basic skills obtained in law school. Mere admission to a state bar is hardly viewed as sufficient to guarantee that the new lawyer possesses the necessary competence with which to advise and represent clients.

It is also true that mere length of time as a lawyer does not
necessarily ensure competence. Almost any lawyer in this
country who has been licensed by a state to practice law,
and has engaged in such practice for three years, can be
admitted to the Supreme Court of the United States, without
further determination as to whether that lawyer is competent to practice before the highest court of this country.

Your right to competence in a lawyer is normally fulfilled by
a lawyer's experience, his basic intelligence, and his ability
to learn from that experience. When combined with
adequate motivation, determination, and dedication, these
factors tend to develop the "wisdom" which is a key element of legal competence. A lawyer's contact with and
guidance by other lawyers more experienced than he, together with a willingness on the part of an inexperienced
lawyer to continue his legal education after law school,
add further to the lawyer's competence and his ability to
properly represent a client.

Few lawyers will readily acknowledge that they are not
competent to handle a particular legal matter. Recognizing
this, the legal profession has concluded that a lawyer is not
representing a client in a competent manner when he: (1)
handles a legal matter which he knows or should know he
is not competent to handle, (2) handles a legal matter without adequate preparation, or, (3) neglects a legal matter
which a client has entrusted to him. It is important that you
attempt to determine, prior to the time you hire the lawyer,
that he has the professional experience needed to provide
the service you require and will work diligently to provide
that service.

How do you determine if the lawyer you intend to hire is
competent to handle your problem? First, you ask questions
and more questions. Second, as a matter of principle, you

should not be satisfied with what you hear from the lawyer about his ability and experience, and you should question the lawyer carefully in this regard. Third, you should check out the lawyer's comments to determine the extent to which they accurately reflect his experience, or whether he may in fact be "puffing" in an effort to get your business. Last, you should expect full and regular communication from your lawyer. One of the most frequent complaints about lawyers is that they neglect their clients or fail to keep them fully informed. As a condition of employing a lawyer, insist, as you have a right to do, that you receive not only monthly itemized billing statements, but also that periodic status report and copies of all correspondence, documents, and pleadings prepared by or received by your lawyer. All of this will aid you in determining whether the lawyer you hired is providing the needed service in a competent and diligent manner.

" 'He was a bad lawyer,' said O'Connell, 'but he was the most sensible looking man talking nonsense he ever saw.'"

Daniel O'Connor
(referring to Lord Manners), Burke,
History of Lord Chancellors of Ireland, 1870, p. 203

Remember, even a lawyer who is competent at the time you hire him may subsequently become incompetent because of a personal, emotional, or physical problem, or for some other reason.

However, your right to competent performance is continuous. It also includes preventing the lawyer you hire from
limiting his liability to you for any legal malpractice which
he may commit. If the lawyer is incompetent, he should not
have accepted the employment and any attempt by that
lawyer to limit his liability should be viewed as an admission that he is incompetent to render the needed service. If
the lawyer you have hired attempts to do this, immediately
begin to search for another more competent one.

CONFIDENTIALITY

Because it is important that you be completely open and
candid with your lawyer, and give your lawyer all the necessary information about your legal problem without fear
that any of that information will be disclosed to others and
possibly used against you, every state recognizes a fundamental obligation imposed on every lawyer to preserve and
protect the confidences and secrets of his clients, as well as
those who have sought to employ the lawyer.

Not only is a lawyer prohibited from revealing a confidence
or secret of his client, or using such a confidence or secret
to the disadvantage of the client, the lawyer is also prohibited from using that confidence or secret for his own advantage, or for the advantage of a third person, unless the client
has consented after full disclosure of all facts relating to the
circumstances under which the disclosure and use of that
confidence or secret is proposed.

However, there are circumstances under which a lawyer
may reveal information pertaining to a confidence or secret
of a client. Generally, these are: (1) when the client consents, after the lawyer has fully explained the need for such
disclosure; (2) when disclosure is necessary for effective

representation of a client; (3) when such disclosure is required by law to prevent the commission of a crime; or (4) when such disclosure is necessary to establish or collect the lawyer's fee or to defend himself, his employees, or his associates against an accusation by the client of wrongful conduct.

How safe, in fact, are your confidences and secrets when given to your lawyer? Most lawyers, be they sole practitioners or members of law firms, maintain one or more files for each client. Into these files go correspondence, pleadings, documents, and other writings which contain information pertaining to the client's legal matters. These files are usually stored in filing cabinets within the lawyer's office. Also, within most law offices are fellow lawyers as well as various non-lawyer personnel such as paralegals, legal secretaries, receptionists, and law clerks. In many law offices, these individuals have unrestricted access to the files of clients as contained in filing cabinets. As such, they have the opportunity to examine the contents of a client's file.

If you are concerned about the true preservation of a confidence or secret which you intend to disclose to your lawyer, carefully and fully discuss with him the manner by which he intends to preserve that confidence or secret, the circumstances under which disclosure may be made, the manner in which the confidence or secret will be protected, who within the lawyer's office will have access to that confidence or secret, and what assurance you can receive to satisfy you that such confidence will, in fact, be preserved.

You should also be aware that any such confidence or secret which you impart to your lawyer may not be disclosed by that lawyer merely because the relationship between you and your lawyer terminates. The lawyer is obligated to preserve such confidence or secret after the termination of his employment. It makes no difference whether the lawyer/client relationship ends by completion of the service needed, discharge, withdrawal, retirement or disability of the lawyer, or the death of one of the parties; the confidence and secrets imparted to the lawyer during the relationship are entitled to protection forever.

A FULL ACCOUNTING

The manner in which lawyers handle money in their possession which is owned by clients, to be paid to the lawyer in the form of legal fees, reimbursement for costs incurred, or through the lawyer to some third party, creates certain obligations on the part of the lawyer and certain rights on the part of the client. Generally, such monies are legal fees, trust funds held and controlled by the lawyer, or monies intended for some third party and temporarily held by the lawyer. Let us consider each of these in turn.

Legal Fees

By agreeing to pay a legal fee in exchange for a needed legal service, you indicate your intent to enter into a transaction similar to many others in which you agree to pay the purchase price for a particular product. And, as in those other obligations, you are entitled to get your money's worth and to know that you are getting your money's worth. In terms of legal services, this means a full and complete accounting by the lawyer providing the service so that you are informed and able to determine, independent of any representations by the lawyer, that the fee you are paying is for a legal service which was needed and performed in a timely and competent fashion. To aid you in obtaining this

120 informed status, you are entitled and have a right to insist that the lawyer providing the service give you the information necessary to make this determination. This means an itemized monthly billing statement, in the format discussed in Chapter Two. Insisting that the lawyer you hire provide you with such a statment, and not paying the lawyer's bill until you received such a statement, will insure a full accounting of the legal fees you incur.

Trust Funds

It is not uncommon for lawyers to act as trustees in the administration of trust funds for the benefit of clients, or their family members, or others. As such, lawyers have access to those funds and have an absolute obligation to act with the highest degree of honesty in the handling of such funds. Most lawyers discharge their duty as a trustee in such a fashion.

But there are instances in which lawyers "co-mingle" and misappropriate monies in trust funds. In some instances, "co-mingling" is in the nature of poor recordkeeping by the lawyer. In other instances such poor recordkeeping is intended to create confusion or otherwise obscure the manner in which the lawyer has misappropriated funds for his own use. As one whose money or other property has been placed in trust with the lawyer, you have a right to insist that the lawyer acting as trustee immediately acknowledge in writing his receipt of such monies or other properties; agree to keep them separate and identifiable; disclose the location, account number, and other pertinent information; and maintain complete and accurate records of all such monies or property while they are in the possession of the lawyer. Additionally, the lawyer should acknowledge, in writing, the circumstances under which such money or property will be distributed or disbursed.

You also have a right to, and should insist on, receipt of photostat copies of the quarterly or other periodic statements of the bank or other savings institution where the money is on deposit, showing the amount of money in the account, as well as any accrued interest or charges affecting the balance. You should also insist that your lawyer provide you with periodic reports on the status of such trust fund monies; the amount in the fund; any disbursements which have occurred since the last report; and any deposits, earnings or other payments which have increased the balance. It is suggested that you receive such reports at least monthly. But bear in mind that no bookkeeping requirements imposed upon a dishonest lawyer will necessarily prevent the misappropriation of trust fund monies. Adequate bookkeeping requirements will promptly notify you of any such misappropriations so you can take immediate action to remove such funds from the control of the lawyer.

Settlement Funds and
Other Monies

There are many ways in which lawyers come into possession of monies belonging to a client. Such monies may represent payments in connection with the settlement of a client's lawsuit, real estate deposits held in escrow, advances by a client in anticipation of costs to be incurred by the lawyer, funds collected from a third party on behalf of the client, prepaid legal fees for services yet to be performed, or monies to be paid for a fine incurred by the client. No matter how your lawyer came into possession of your money, you as the client are entitled to an immediate acknowledgment in writing by the lawyer that he has recieved such monies on your behalf, and the circumstances upon which those monies will be disbursed either to you or on your behalf. If it is anticipated that the lawyer will hold such monies for more than a few days, insist on the periodic report mentioned above.

"No man can serve two masters; for either he will hate the one, and love the other; or else he will hold to the one, and despise the other."

Matthew 6:24

AN UNDIVIDED EFFORT FOR YOUR BENEFIT

You have the right to insist that the lawyer you hire, independent of his own interests, those of his other clients, or those of third persons, exercise independent professional judgment solely for your benefit and free from any and all compromising influences or loyalties.

This right to an undivided effort from your lawyer is generally referred to as the conflict of interest rule. Your lawyer is faced with three alternatives when he knows or suspects that his representation of you has created a conflict of interest: (1) to inform you and all other interested clients of the conflict and possible consequences if he continues to represent all parties, and continue to represent all parties only after receiving the expressed and informed consent from each; (2) to withdraw from the representation of all but one of the clients, after informing all parties of the conflict; or (3) to withdraw from the representation of all of the parties. If your lawyer continues to represent you or one of the other interested parties, and one or more of the other interested parties complains, the lawyer will bear the burden of demonstrating that his decision was a fair one.

It is not uncommon for this conflict of interest problem to arise where a lawyer, motivated by a desire to receive a fee, agrees to accept or continue in the employ of a particular client despite his knowledge or suspicion that such employment constitutes a conflict. A lawyer's desire for financial security may cause him to overlook such a conflict and when this happens, it is the client, not the lawyer, who usually suffers.

This may also be true in situations where a client is foolish enough to permit the lawyer to obtain a direct economic interest in the client's business, such as where a lawyer obtains an ownership position in the client's business in exchange for providing legal advice. While at first blush such an arrangement may be viewed in a favorable light by the client, as a means to avoid the payment of legal fees, it invariably results in the client having doubt as to whether the lawyer is providing legal advice which is for the benefit of the client or in the best interest of the lawyer from the financial standpoint of the lawyer's involvement in the client's business.

Still other examples involve situations where lawyers have a social or political interest adverse to the clients's position and the lawyer's advice is tempered or otherwise affected by such social or political consideration. As a a client, you have a right to a lawyer's loyalty to you, undiluted by any personal interests on the part of the lawyer, irrespective of whether it is financial, social, or political in nature.

If you know or suspect that your lawyer is involved in a conflict of interest affecting the matter for which you sought his services, you should immediately insist that your lawyer demonstrate, in writing, that the conflict does not exist, or that he inform you, in writing, of the full extent of the conflict, so that you can make an informed decision as to whether to permit the lawyer to continue in his representation of you. In such instances, you should feel no hesitancy to contact another lawyer and confer with him as to whether the conflict of interest is such that it appears advisable to replace your original lawyer.

WRITTEN EXPLANATIONS
AND OPINIONS

Much of the advice rendered by lawyers to their clients is done in face-to-face meetings and in telephone conversations. Some is done in writing in the form of letters from the lawyer to the client. You have the right to determine how you will receive such advice and should not hesitate to ask that such advice be in writing whenever you wish to have a record of it.

Any lawyer rendering competent professional advice will not hesitate to put such advice in writing on request. Reluctance or refusal of a lawyer to reduce to writing the advice given a client is usually an indication that the lawyer has not adequately familiarized himself with the facts surrounding the client's legal problem and the applicable law.

From your standpoint, as the one who is expected to pay the lawyer's bill for such advice, you are entitled to receive it in the form you, and not the lawyer, determine. You should be especially concerned with a lawyer who is willing to give you advice verbally, but who will not, for one reason or another, reduce it to writing.

LANGUAGE YOU UNDERSTAND 125

In an effort to assist people to understand written agreements they are frequently asked to sign in consumer related transactions for personal, family, or household purposes, a number of states have either enacted or are considering the enactment of so-called "Plain English" statutes. Designed to require the use of words having common everyday meanings, the existence and consideration of such statutes highlight a serious problem.

Too often, a lawyer will communicate with a client by way of a writing containing legal terms or phrases not understood by the client. If your lawyer uses a legal term or phrase, or any other terminology which you do not fully understand, you have a right to insist that it be defined. If you are asked to sign an agreement prepared by your lawyer, or a lawyer for some other party to the transaction, insist that any such words be defined and that the definition be set forth *in the agreement or other writing*.

There are a number of excellent dictionaries, including Black's Law Dictionary published by West Publishing Company, which are available to assist you in obtaining the definition of legal terms and phrases. These dictionaries are generally available in city and county public law libraries as well as in most book stores.

PARTICIPATION IN
DECISION-MAKING

The luxury of having a lawyer contact a client in each instance where a decision must be made, and discussing with the client all relevant considerations pertaining to that decision, is an unrealistic expectation. But as a lawyer's client, you are entitled to participate in all decision-making which affects the merits of your legal matter, or may substantially prejudice one or more of your rights. It is your lawyer's duty to exercise his best effort to insure that you make an informed decision concerning your legal matter.

It is not uncommon for a client's claim to result in a settlement offer by an opposing party. A decision must then be made whether to accept or reject it. In the final analysis, it is the client, not the laywer, who decides whether a settlement offer should be accepted. But the lawyer should provide as much information as possible about those factors which will aid the client in making such a decision.

Remember, as the one paying for the legal services provided, you are entitled to participate in the decision-making process as those services are provided. This right to participate in decision-making should be clearly established at the outset of the lawyer/client relationship. With respect to the acceptance or rejection of settlement offers in particular, it is a good idea to obtain a written acknowledgment from your lawyer that in addition to disclosing any and all settlement offers received, no acceptance or rejection of any such offer will occur without your expressed approval after your full and complete participation in the discussion concerning any such offer.

RECORDKEEPING AND ACCESS TO YOUR FILES

Typically, a client's legal matters in the form of correspondence, pleadings, documents, and other writings will be collected into one or more files labeled with the client's name and other identifying marks such as a file code or number. In this manner, the lawyer will have ready access to information pertaining to a particular client.

It is important to bear in mind that the writings which go 127
into such a file are usually prepared by the lawyer for the
benefit of his client, and it is the client who pays for their
preparation. The client therefore has every right to insist
that his file be maintained in a fashion acceptable to the
client and that it be made available to the client on reasonable request.

The manner in which the lawyer you hire intends to maintain a file pertaining to you should be discussed with him
before he is hired. At that time, you should also discuss and
secure the lawyer's approval to allow you access, on reasonable notice, to examine the file.

If you are careful in the selection of the lawyer you hire, and
insist on monthly itemized billing statements; periodic
status reports; and copies of all correspondence, documents, pleadings, and other writings prepared by or received by your lawyer, you should have little need to
examine the file maintained by your lawyer. That file
should be nothing more than a duplicate of information
which you have received at more or less the same time it
was received by your lawyer.

DISCHARGING
YOUR LAWYER

One very important right, which many clients do not
realize they have, is the absolute right, at any time, to discharge their lawyer, with or without cause. It makes no
difference whether you have a written or oral employment
or fee agreement with your lawyer, you still have a right to
discharge him. However, if you do so without a valid
cause, you may have an obligation to pay your lawyer the
reasonable value of the services he rendered up to the date

he was discharged by you. What constitutes valid cause varies from state to state but generally, misconduct by your lawyer is sufficient cause for such discharge.

Because the relationship between a lawyer and client is deemed to be confidential and personal, one which no one has a right to know about other than the lawyer and the client, it is considered too important a relationship to be subjected to the evils which might arise if a client were forced to continue using a lawyer the client did not trust. This is the reason you have a right to discharge your lawyer at any time.

The decision to discharge a lawyer should not be made lightly. Such a discharge will likely result in the need to replace the discharged lawyer and this may take time, energy, and expense. Even assuming the discharged lawyer performed in a unsatisfactory manner up to the point of discharge, the new lawyer will have to familiarize himself with what the discharged lawyer has accomplished, and this will mean additional expense to you. There is also the matter of deciding whether or not to compensate the discharged lawyer for services rendered to the date of discharge.

It is a good idea to first consult with another lawyer before discharging your original lawyer. You should have no hesitancy in this regard. Contrary to the public image that lawyers stick together, most lawyers are concerned about allegations of misconduct among their fellow lawyers.

By conferring with another laywer, you can receive needed advice on your obligation, if any, to the lawyer you intend to discharge, and also the assurance that your new lawyer will assist you in protecting your rights during the transition period, which will include obtaining your files, records, documents, and other materials in the possession or under the control of the lawyer you discharge. Any lawyer so discharged has the obligation to take reasonable steps to avoid any foreseeable prejudice to you by such discharge and the lawyer is also obligated to return promptly any unearned fee paid by you in advance.

ADDITIONAL PROTECTION TO CONSIDER

Sometimes the best effort in securing the best available lawyer to provide a needed service is not sufficient. Even the best of lawyers will make mistakes on occasion, and when they do, the client usually suffers. Whether the lawyer also suffers is of little consolation to a client who has been damaged by such a mistake. To protect against the human element in the lawyer's performance of needed services, you may wish to consider requesting the additional protection of legal malpractice insurance and/or a performance bond.

Legal Malpractice Insurance

Malpractice claims against lawyers have risen sharply in recent years and one report indicates the claim rate during a three-year period ending in 1975 increased from approximately one claim per forty lawyers to one claim per thirty lawyers. This apparent trend, coupled with estimates suggesting that one lawyer in every ten will soon face a malpractice claim, is as startling to lawyers as it should be to you.

No one knows the total number of lawyers who have committed legal malpractice. Nor do we know the total amount

130 of damages that clients have suffered as a result of such malpractice. Those insurance companies who have offered legal malpractice insurance and maintained accurate statistics on the resulting claims no doubt have some idea of the extent to which such claims are asserted. But since those insurance companies usually write insurance only for lawyers who are qualified (i.e., low-risk applicants), even those statistics would not tell the entire story. Many lawyers simply do not carry such insurance, cannot afford the premiums charged, or are unable to obtain such insurance. It is probably the lawyers in this last category, (i.e., those who cannot obtain malpractice insurance) who are most likely to commit acts of malpractice resulting in damage to their clients.

"The law is the only profession which records its mistakes carefully, exactly as they occur, and yet does not identify them as mistakes."

Elliott Dunlap Smith
39 J. M. Jud. Soc, 47 (1954)

If the lawyer you hire commits an act of malpractice resulting in damage to you, you have the alternatives of: (1) doing nothing, (2) convincing your lawyer to reimburse you, (3) filing a lawsuit against your lawyer, and/or (4) filing a claim with the insurance company which issued your lawyer's malpractice insurance.

Taking no action is obviously unacceptable. Convincing
your lawyer to reimburse you is unlikely since it is usually
the lawyer with the least financial responsibility who is
most likely to commit malpractice. Competent lawyers
have little difficulty in securing clients willing to pay for
competent services and as such are usually financially responsible. If you select the third alternative of filing a lawsuit against the lawyer, there are many obstacles in your
path. You must find another lawyer willing to pursue the
claim, pay that lawyer to do so, and hope that you will end
up with a judgment. Then you must attempt to satisfy that
judgment, and this can only be done if the lawyer has
assets which are reachable. The whole process of obtaining
and satisfying a judgment against a lawyer can take years.

Filing a claim for damages resulting from your lawyer's
malpractice requires, of course, that your lawyer was or is
covered by a form of malpractice insurance applicable to
your claim.

Generally, legal malpractice is a lawyer's failure to measure
up to a required standard of care (commonly referred to as
negligence) or a required standard of conduct. The terms
and conditions under which coverage is provided by a
malpractice insurance policy vary greatly, depending on
the insurance company issuing the policy, the terms of the
policy, the past history of the insured lawyer, and the nature
of the lawyer's practice. Determining whether your claim
comes within the terms and conditions of a particular policy is a job for a competent lawyer.

Few clients exhibit the foresight to ask whether a particular
lawyer under consideration for employment does in fact
offer a client the protection of legal malpractice insurance.
But after the discussion above, it should be clear that asking

about legal malpractice insurance and insisting that the lawyer you hire have such insurance will help you to protect yourself against an act of legal malpractice resulting in damage to you.

While making such inquiry of the lawyer you are considering for employment may sound extreme, consider for a moment the situation where you are faced with a substantial legal problem, the mishandling of which will result in a severely adverse financial impact on you. If such mishandling constitutes legal malpractice, having satisfied yourself that the lawyer you hired has legal malpractice insurance may well give you the additional protection you need.

Being human, a lawyer is as susceptible as anyone else to making a mistake. And not all mistakes by lawyers are made by those who are sole practitioners. There have been numerous cases in which members of some of the most prestigious law firms in this country have committed legal malpractice resulting in severe damage to their clients. No doubt there are many more instances in which legal malpractice claims are quietly settled and therefore never brought to the public's attention.

For your own protection, ask the following questions of the lawyer you are considering hiring:

- Does the law firm with which you are associated have such insurance?
- Do you have legal malpractice insurance?
- Is such insurance applicable to your work on my behalf?
- What are the inclusive dates during which such insurance is applicable?
- What is the name of the insurance company which issued the policy?

- What is the insurance policy number?
- Will you describe the extent of coverage offered by such policy?
- What acts or conduct are not covered by such insurance?
- Will you advise me promptly if your policy is cancelled?

Faithful Performance Bond

The best protection against damage from the misconduct of one's lawyer comes from the careful evaluation and informed selection of that lawyer in the first instance. The next best protection is to ensure that your lawyer has legal malpractice insurance. But on occasion, a client will ask a lawyer to act in some non-lawyer capacity and if the lawyer agrees, his conduct is likely to be outside the scope of the protection offered by his legal malpractice insurance. The most common examples of a lawyer acting in a non-lawyer capacity are those which relate to a lawyer acting as trustee in the management and disposition of a client's assets, as a guardian of a client's minor child, or as executor of a client's estate on the client's death. While state laws vary as to the requirement that one acting in the capacity of trustee, guardian, or executor post a bond to ensure faithful performance, few clients exhibit the foresight to make the necessary inquiry of a lawyer as to the requirement or availability of such a bond.

Just as many companies engaged in the handling of monies and securities, such as banks and savings and loan associations, frequently obtain fiduciary bonds to protect themselves against loss from the want of honesty, integrity or fidelity on the part of their employees, so too can a client many times obtain additional protection by what can generally be described as a faithful performance bond. While no client would intentionally ask a lawyer he did not trust

134   to act as trustee, guardian, or executor, there are occasions
when lawyers, like others, are subject to various financial,
emotional, or other pressures which result in a client or
others sustaining damage by the unfaithful performance of
that lawyer. How can you best protect yourself against such
an event?

Before making a decision on whether to have your lawyer
act in a non-lawyer capacity, ask your lawyer the following
questions:

- Is it possible to obtain a bond to ensure faithful performance of the duties you will undertake?
- What is the procedure for obtaining such a bond?
- What is the cost of such a bond?
- For what period will such a bond remain in effect?
- Is there any conduct which would not be protected by such a bond?
- If I want further information on such a bond, whom should I consult?
- Will you obtain a copy of such a bond so I can review its terms?

In addition to the information you will get from your lawyer's response to the questions above, consider contacting your local insurance agent, bond broker, or banker, for such additional inquiry as you feel is necessary.

Client Security Funds

As we discussed earlier, there are numerous situations in which lawyers hold monies belonging to their clients. If a lawyer misappropriates these monies, as happens from time to time, the client who is entitled to those monies is damaged and may not be able to successfully pursue a claim against the lawyer for reimbursement. The reason for this should be obvious. Lawyers who misappropriate monies belonging to their clients usually do so because they need money and are usually unable to financially respond to a client's demand for reimbursement.

To aid clients who have been victimized in this manner, all but two states (Utah and Wisconsin) have created what have come to be known as client security funds. Often administered by trustees appointed by the highest court of the state or selected by a governing body of the state bar association, these funds are usually financed by appropriations from state bar dues paid by lawyers or fees assessed against lawyers and specifically designated for the fund. By this means, all lawyers contribute to the reimbursement of funds misappropriated by a dishonest lawyer. The extent of such reimbursement varies from state to state but generally ranges from $5,000 or less per individual claim to upwards of $200,000 or more for claims resulting from a course of misconduct by any one lawyer. Whether a particular claim is satisfied by payment from the fund is generally made on the basis of merit.

If you believe you have a claim which qualifies for payment from such a fund, contact a lawyer or write to your state bar association (Appendix B) or call or write to the local bar association in your community and make inquiry.

It should be noted that the best way to protect against a lawyer's misappropriation of monies belonging to you is to make a thorough investigation of the lawyer you intend to hire, insist upon the disclosures pertaining to such monies which we discussed above, and, as we show in Chapter Five, periodically evaluate your lawyer's performance.

136   AFTER THE LAWYER/CLIENT RELATIONSHIP: YOUR CONTINUING RIGHTS

No matter how the relationship with your lawyer ends, he owes you, as a former client, an obligation not to represent another client if that representation will require the undoing of the work the lawyer did for you, or would otherwise require use or possible use of information received confidentially from you, during the relationship, or could otherwise create an appearance of impropriety.

In other words, once a lawyer/client relationship has been created, the lawyer is faced with certain clear obligations to you forever.

5 The Need To Periodically Evaluate Your Lawyer

Do not be lulled into a false sense of security by believing that once you have hired a lawyer he will always perform in a timely and competent manner. Many of those who have occasion to use a lawyer know otherwise.

All too frequently, lawyers promise prompt action on a client's legal problem but fail to carry through on such promises. Much of the criticism of lawyers centers on their failure to perform the services for which they were hired in a timely enough fashion. Additional criticism is often directed at lawyers for failing to keep their clients informed of how the client's legal matter is progressing. Additional criticism centers on excessive fees, failure to respond to inquiries by the client as to the status of the client's matter, unexplained delays in solving the client's problem, and unpreparedness on the part of the lawyer.

In nearly all such instances, had the client conducted a comprehensive periodic evaluation of the lawyer hired, and immediately brought to that lawyer's attention any noted or suspected deficiencies, the likelihood of criticism would have been greatly reduced. Periodic evaluation is essential to the maintenance of the lawyer/client relationship at a high point of mutual satisfaction.

Members of the public who hire professionals such as lawyers and doctors to perform needed services do not usually think in terms of evaluating that professional's performance. They are generally content to rely on a belief that the needed service will be performed in a competent manner, and such reliance is a risk. Fortunately, most professionals perform competently, but some do not, and it is with these that we must be concerned. Just as the senior partners in a law firm will periodically conduct a formal or informal review of the young lawyers acting as associates in the firm, so too must a client evaluate his lawyer.

"The fact that a lawyer advises such foolish conduct does not relieve it of its foolishness."

Judge Emery
in *Hanscom* vs. *Marston,* 82 Me. 288, 298 (1890)

This is no easy task since the client is usually unfamiliar with the intricacies of the lawyer's profession, special training, and experience. After all, it was because of these factors that the lawyer was hired in the first place. But even the most competent of lawyers can be subjected to personal, financial, marital, or family problems, or other problems which have an effect on the lawyer's ability to perform in a competent fashion. Depending on the severity of the lawyer's personal problems, and the length of time over which legal services are to be rendered, the effect such personal problems have on the lawyer's ability to render competent services may be substantial.

140   Given this, it is suggested that an evaluation be conducted
       not less than once every three months during the period
       your lawyer is providing services. Depending on the nature
       of your legal problem, its importance to you, and the effect
       of an adverse outcome on you, you may want to conduct
       such an evaluation even more frequently. You should begin
       your evaluation by recalling your original objectives when
       seeking out the services of a lawyer. It is a good idea to
       review the original notes you took during your first meeting
       with your lawyer, and then proceed to ask youself the fol-
       lowing questions to determine if your lawyer is performing
       up to par.

QUESTIONS TO ASK YOURSELF
IN EVALUATING YOUR LAWYER

■ Does my lawyer appear to be prepared when matters
pertaining to my legal needs arise?

Whether it be the preparation of a will, a written contract,
or a matter for trial, the key to a lawyer's successful handling of any client matter is thorough preparation. Failure to
provide a written agreement when promised, appearing unfamiliar with facts which were previously brought to the
lawyer's attention, failing to carry out actions requested by
you, or providing excuses for the nonperformance of a requested service, are all indications that the lawyer you
hired is not functioning satisfactorily.

■ Is my lawyer performing in the manner originally represented?

Recalling your original objectives in hiring a lawyer and the
assurances you insisted your lawyer give you (that he would
be prompt, expeditious, etc.), compare those objectives

and assurances with his actual performance. Most lawyers need no motivation to perform properly, but for those who do, the importance of a client insisting on such performance cannot be overemphasized. Remember, you hired a lawyer to work for you, not to tell you that he was too busy handling someone else's business to attend to yours.

- Is my lawyer continuing to exhibit interest and concern about my legal problems?

Not uncommonly, a lawyer in need of legal business will exhibit great interest when a prospective client discusses a legal problem and indicates a desire to hire the lawyer. Too often the lawyer's interest evaporates once he has been hired and legal fees begin to come rolling in. Honest expressions of interest and concern about your legal problems are best exhibited by a lawyer who not only promises to perform the needed service, but does in fact perform the service to the satisfactory solution of your problem.

- Is my lawyer keeping me informed of progress on the handling of my legal problem?

Promises to keep you informed about the handling of your legal matter often go unkept once you have agreed to hire the lawyer. The single most common cause of complaints about lawyers is that the lawyer failed to keep the client informed of what, if anything, the lawyer was doing to solve the client's legal problem. This is a serious problem and one for which the legal profession has yet to determine a solution. However, your solution is simple. As we discussed above, *you should insist on monthly itemized billing statements, periodic status reports, and copies of all correspondence, documents, pleadings and other writings prepared by or received by your lawyer.* Additionally, you should secure free access to the files pertaining to your legal matter as maintained by your lawyer and insist on access to your lawyer as frequently as necessary to have him explain any matter to you, or otherwise report progress on the handling of your problem.

■ Is my lawyer being honest in his dealings with me?

Critical to a satisfactory lawyer/client relationship is the belief that the lawyer you hired is honest both in what he says to you and the way in which he handles your affairs. Any doubt about your lawyer's honesty should be resolved immediately. If you suspect that the lawyer you hire is acting dishonestly, you should immediately confront him, and discuss the matter fully. If you are not satisfied with the lawyer's explanation, immediately take steps to remove him from any and all positions from which he can inflict damage on you by his dishonesty.

■ Is my lawyer being fair and reasonable in charging for his legal services?

Again, recall your original discussion with the lawyer regarding fees. Also, review your fee agreement to determine whether the charges are in accordance with the agreement, or have been increased by the lawyer without your permission. Your insistence upon and receipt of itemized monthly billing statements will greatly assist you in answering this question. As to any costs which are being incurred, you first should have been informed of such costs and have given your consent in accordance with the procedure you and your lawyer originally agreed upon.

■ Are my legal needs being satisfied?

In hiring your lawyer, you acknowledged the need for a legal service and instructed the lawyer to provide that service. Now, with some time having elapsed since the lawyer was hired, it is important to determine whether he is in fact providing that service.

Too many lawyers exhibit great energies in obtaining clients only to fail to show similar energies in solving the client's problem. The lawyer you hire should be able to recognize potential legal problems before they develop into actual ones so that you can avoid them. It is not possible to recognize all potential legal problems, but a competent lawyer is usually the best person to detect a potential legal problem, and you should expect him to keep you regularly informed in this regard.

■ How does my lawyer compare with other lawyers?

Occasionally, a client will come in contact with lawyers representing other parties to the same legal dispute which necessitated the client's hiring of a lawyer. When this happens, it provides the client with an excellent opportunity to compare the lawyer he hired with those other lawyers. This can be done in such areas as the degree of preparation, performance, communication skills, interest, general appearance, and the like. Many times, it is not that difficult for a non-lawyer (i.e., yourself) to detect differences in ability among lawyers involved in providing legal services to their respective clients in the same legal problem.

■ If I had another legal problem, would I hire the same lawyer?

This is a question which many clients put off answering until after the lawyer has completed his work and the legal problem has been resolved. Too many clients have learned to their regret that delay in facing up to a mistake in hiring a lawyer can only add to their problems. It does little good to wait until the lawyer has completed his work before answering this question. If you know or suspect that the lawyer is not performing adequately, you had better give serious thought to correcting the situation immediately. Delay will only result in damage to you, not the lawyer who is performing inadequately.

WHAT TO DO
IF YOUR EVALUATION
INDICATES A PROBLEM

Having conducted your evaluation, and having detected a problem or possible problem in your lawyer's performance, it is important that you act promptly. Far too many clients know or suspect the existence of a problem with their lawyer but refrain from taking action to solve that problem. Many times this is due to a belief that nothing can be done once the lawyer has been hired, and that any insistence by the client on improved performance by the lawyer is likely to further damage the relationship, to the client's detriment.

True, telling your lawyer that he has not kept certain promises he made at the outset of the relationship, or that his performance appears to be deficient, or his legal fees excessive, or that you suspect he has acted in a dishonest manner may well cause deterioration of the relationship. But the alternative is to take no action, let the lawyer continue with his deficient performance or other misconduct, and know that you, not the lawyer, will suffer as a result.

"The first thing we do, let's kill all the lawyers."

William Shakespeare

The legal profession has yet to determine an effective way of dealing with all the levels of lawyer misconduct. In aggravated cases such as misappropriation of a client's trust fund monies, or other criminal conduct, reasonably prompt disciplinary action is instituted against the lawyer. But in many instances when a lawyer is guilty of lesser misconduct, such as the failure to perform a needed service quickly enough, misrepresenting an important fact affecting the client's legal matter, or continuing to represent a client while knowing that a conflict of interest exists, disciplinary action against the lawyer is either nonexistent or too late in coming to benefit the injured client. Until, and unless, the legal profession becomes much more effective in dealing with misconduct on the part of its members, it will continue to be necessary for clients to look out for themselves.

Just as it is no easy task for a client to effectively evaluate his lawyer's performance, it is also no easy task for that client to deal with a poor evaluation of his lawyer. There are no hard and fast rules on how a client should proceed, and each problem with a lawyer must be considered individually in the context of the lawyer/client relationship, the personalities involved, the needs of the client, and a multitude of other factors. The following procedure is offered merely as a guideline for dealing with the problems ensuing from a negative evaluation:

Step No. 1:

Write out a clear statement of the problem in as detailed a manner as possible. For example, if the problem centers on a lack of adequate communication between you and your lawyer, or the lawyer's repeated failure to return calls you have placed to him, try to note the day of each unreturned call or request for information and the reason you had for calling.

Step No. 2:

Write out each question you have regarding the problem which you want to ask your lawyer. In this way, you will be sure to include all your questions regarding the matter. Having written them out, you will lessen the chance for an oversight when meeting with the lawyer to discuss the matter.

Step No. 3:

Contact your lawyer and arrange a mutually convenient time for a face-to-face meeting. If your lawyer is opposed to meeting with you and wants to discuss the problem over the telephone, advise him that you want a face-to-face meeting and insist upon it. If you are unable to schedule a meeting with your lawyer, send the lawyer a certified mail letter, or telegram, indicating your desire for a meeting and specifying a date and time for that meeting and advising that unless you are immediately notified of an alternative date and time, you will expect the meeting to proceed as you have scheduled it.

Step No. 4:

Attend the scheduled meeting with the attitude that you are sincere in your desire to resolve the problem, being sure to take your written statement of the problem and your written questions to the meeting for reference. Discuss the problem fully with your lawyer, being sure to get your lawyer's viewpoint as well. Attempt to reach a workable solution to the problem, being sure that you will receive the high level of performance promised when you hired him.

Step No. 5:

Following the meeting, mail to your lawyer a letter in which you refer to the meeting, the problem discussed, and the agreement or lack of agreement for resolving that problem. In this way, you will again impress upon your lawyer the seriousness with which you view the problem and the importance you place upon the agreement with your lawyer to resolve it. An example of such a letter appears below. It is a good idea to send a copy of such a letter to the senior partner in the law firm as this will further impress upon the lawyer to whom the letter is addressed your intent that the problem be resolved. Be sure you keep a copy of your letter for future reference should the need arise.

June—, 19—

LAW OFFICES OF
[insert law firm name and address]

Dear [insert lawyer's name]:

The purpose of this letter is to confirm the outcome of our meeting in your office on [insert date of meeting].

I requested the meeting to discuss the problem which arose regarding [insert nature of problem]. You acknowledged the problem's existence, and assured me that you would take immediate action to correct this matter and prevent its reoccurrence.

You also assured me my legal service needs will be handled by you in a prompt and efficient manner.

Please keep me fully advised of all developments pertaining to my legal matter.

Sincerely,
JOHN DOE

JD/ms

copy to: [senior or managing partner of law firm, if applicable]

However, what if an agreement was not reached to resolve the problem, or despite such agreement, the problem persists? In such a case, the following additional steps are suggested:

Step No. 6:

Notify your lawyer in writing by certified mail with return receipt requested, or telegram, with delivery confirmed, that the problem persists despite your meeting, and request that the problem be resolved immediately. In your letter or telegram, request that your lawyer acknowledge receipt in writing and indicate a willingness to comply with your request to resolve the problem immediately.

Step No. 7:

If you fail to receive such an acknowledgment as indicated in Step No. 6, promptly consult another lawyer with whom you can confer regarding your legal matter and the problem with your lawyer. Find out your status regarding possible damage stemming from the problem's irresolution, fee obligation if your original lawyer is discharged, and whether or not you have any basis for a claim against your lawyer based on the quality of his performance.

Step No. 8:

Discharge your original lawyer in the manner recommended by the lawyer with whom you have now conferred and hired. Request that your new lawyer obtain a return of all records or other documents which your original lawyer may still have, and ask your new lawyer to give you a written opinion, as soon as possible, as to the status of your legal matter at the time your original lawyer was discharged, as well as any fee obligation which you may have with your original lawyer at the time of such discharge. Also ask your new lawyer to advise you on a recommended course of action in dealing with both the discharge of your original lawyer and the handling of your legal matter.

Step No. 9:

After conferring with your new lawyer, decide whether you wish to lodge with the local or state bar association a formal letter of complaint against your discharged lawyer. The following is an example of such a letter.

June—, 19—

STATE BAR ASSOCIATION OF—
[insert address of bar association]

Gentlemen:
    I employed [insert name and address of lawyer] to act as my lawyer for the purpose of [insert specific reference to reason lawyer employed].
    Contrary to the representations made to me at the time of his employment, [insert lawyer's name] has not performed as promised. Specifically, he has failed to [specify lawyer's misconduct].
    The purpose of this letter is to advise you of the foregoing, lodge a formal complaint against [insert lawyer's name], and request that you take action to discipline him.
    Please acknowledge receipt of this letter and advise me of the action you will take.

Sincerely,

JOHN DOE

JD/ms

copy to: [insert lawyer's name]
        [insert local bar association name and address]
        [insert Better Business Bureau and address]

The discipline of a lawyer is usually administered by the highest court of the state in which the lawyer is admitted to practice law. Generally speaking, a lawyer is subject to discipline when he is convicted of a felony or misdemeanor involving moral turpitude, wilfully disobeys or violates a court order, violates his oath as a lawyer, fails to pay or deliver, after demand, money or property to a client, makes a corrupt or unauthorized appearance on behalf of a client, or is otherwise found to have acted in an unprofessional or unethical manner in violation of the canons and ethics of the legal profession.

Typically, receipt by the local or state bar association of a client or former client's complaint results in referring the complaint to an individual or committee for determination as to its merit. If investigation indicates disciplinary action is needed, the matter is then referred to the court as to the nature and imposition of discipline, which usually takes one of the following forms:

Private Reprimand:

The mildest form of discipline, such a reprimand is usually applied informally and constitutes an admonishment to the lawyer to properly conduct himself. It also establishes a record in case of further misconduct by the lawyer.

Public Reprimand:

Discipline in this form is entered in the public record of the court and is also frequently published in legal publications and newspapers. It is a more severe expression by the court of disapproval of the lawyer's conduct than is a private reprimand and also establishes a record in case of further misbehavior.

Suspension:

A lawyer subjected to suspension may not, during the term of suspension, practice law. Such discipline thus inflicts both a professional and financial penalty and may range from a few days to a year or more. Typically, a suspended lawyer must first establish to the satisfaction of the court ordering the suspension that he has regained good moral character and should be readmitted to the practice of law.

Disbarment:

The most severe form of discipline, disbarment means the taking away of a lawyer's right to practice law. Such discipline is normally reserved for the most serious cases involving a lawyer's criminal misconduct or gross misconduct bordering on a criminal act.

Depending on the severity of the problem and the damage you have sustained, you may also wish to bring a lawsuit against the discharged lawyer for malpractice, in an effort to recover your damages. This should be fully discussed with your new lawyer before such action is initiated.

It is not pleasant to think of taking steps so severe as the discharge and lodging of a formal complaint against a person you have hired to perform a service. But the continued use of a lawyer who has engaged in misconduct will invariably expose you to greater damage than that which you faced when first realizing your need for a legal service and contacting the lawyer. Remember, you hired the lawyer to provide a needed legal service in solving a problem. If that service has not been provided properly, and the problem continues, it is you, not the lawyer, who will suffer.

None of us like to admit that we have made a mistake in
the selection of an individual to provide a needed service,
but it is far better to acknowledge that mistake promptly,
and do something about it, than it is to continue with a
lawyer engaged in misconduct. In fact, your prompt action
in such a situation will constitute a public service by bring-
ing to the attention of those responsible members of the
legal profession the misconduct of the lawyer. In this manner, others who might otherwise be subjected to the lawyer's misconduct will benefit by your action.

Being assured through your periodic evaluations that your
lawyer is doing his job well is the first and best step toward
preventing legal problems from reaching the litiginous and
expensive state. And, though it may sound strange to advise
using a lawyer to prevent legal problems, it is exactly
analogous to advising regular medical checkups to prevent
illness from progressing unseen and therefore unchecked.

6 Preventive Law: A Concept for You

LAWYERS, THE LAW, AND YOU

There are literally millions of laws already enacted and tens of thousands of new laws are enacted each year. Not all of these laws are necessary, well considered by legislative bodies, enacted at the appropriate time or free from different interpretations and effect. The enactment of some laws is the result of public-minded legislators while other laws are enacted as the result of pressure from special interest groups. In theory, all such laws are intended to systemize the rules of social interaction and regulate the conduct of both individuals and businesses in our society. In practice, the effect of all these laws is to subject nearly everyone, at some time during their life, to the need to consult with a lawyer. Indeed, even one's death can cause a lawyer's services to be needed.

In fact, studies have indicated that some two-thirds of all adults in the United States have consulted with a lawyer at least once. Despite this awesome statistic, most people no doubt dislike thinking in terms of needing or hiring a lawyer. The very thought means legal fees and spending money. If a lawyer's services are believed to be necessary, it is a natural reaction for most people to consider an alternative. Initial and apparent "success" in this effort can often be misleading.

EFFORTS TO AVOID
LEGAL FEES

With the ever-increasing cost of legal services, it is no wonder many people mistakenly believe that avoiding a lawyer means avoiding legal fees. Even when faced with a serious legal problem, many people delay in hiring a lawyer in the mistaken belief that such delay will help to hold down legal fees until the time when the lawyer must be consulted.

The irony of such efforts, no matter how well intentioned, is that they *nearly always increase* legal fees. Lawyers have known for years that most of the legal problems they handle, and from which they earn handsome fees, could have been resolved much less expensively if only the client had consulted the lawyer sooner.

All too often, a delay in obtaining legal services gives a "small" legal-service need time to develop into a "large" legal problem. Resolving it then requires additional effort on the part of the lawyer, and in the end it is the client who pays for this additional effort in the form of legal fees. In many instances, a timely telephone conversation or a short meeting with a competent lawyer would have resulted in avoiding the legal problem entirely.

It is this failure to take timely action that frequently hurts the client most. Such a failure can generally be traced to one or more of the "six common mistakes" which have become so familiar to lawyers. It is precisely these mistakes, made repeatedly by people in need of legal services, which should be avoided, not lawyers.

COMMON MISTAKE NO. 1:
Believing Self-Help Is the Best Way to Take Care of a Legal Problem

The old adage "one who acts as his own lawyer has a fool for a client" is still true. Even for a lawyer faced with his own legal problem, self-help is inadvisable. Many of the handsome fees earned by lawyers have been the result of initial attempts by clients to solve their own legal problems. Examples of this abound and include the common situation of a client's writing a contract and then finding out, after a dispute has arisen, that he "forgot" to include a requirement that the losing party pay the legal fees of the prevailing party. Such a clause, had it been inserted, may well have prevented the dispute from arising in the first place, and at least provided for reimbursement of the legal fees incurred. Still other examples include situations where one negotiates the settlement of a claim with an insurance company without first being fully informed as to his legal rights, thereby signing a release that gives away such rights for inadequate consideration. Another example is the writing of one's own will, where a no contest clause prohibiting a fight among various heirs is "forgotten." After the person dies, should one or more of the heirs contest the will, a substantial portion of the estate will end up as legal fees rather than as your legacy to the heirs intended as recipients.

COMMON MISTAKE NO. 2:
Relying on a Friend's Advice in Lieu of Consulting a Lawyer

Many people consult friends and rely on their advice. Whether in a hurry for an answer to a question about a legal problem, not knowing a lawyer to contact, being un-

familiar about how to go about finding a lawyer, or merely
wanting to avoid paying for the advice of a lawyer, the
result is the same: potential disaster.

Although the friend may be well-intentioned in providing
sought-after advice, there is a substantial risk that such a
friend, being untrained in law and the means by which one
can respond to legal problems, will overlook important
rights of the individual, neglect to consider applicable laws,
or even, in all innocence, cause irrevocable injury to the
"friend in need."

COMMON MISTAKE NO. 3:
Avoiding Lawyers
in Order to Avoid Legal Fees

Precisely because the cost of legal advice is so high, one
should consult a lawyer. The common threat connecting
each of the various common mistakes we are discussing is
that they are nearly always motivated, at least in part, by a
desire to avoid legal fees. But payment to a lawyer for an
hour or so of his time, whatever his hourly rate, is usually
far better than getting involved in a dispute such as a lawsuit which then requires a lawyer to expend hundreds or
thousands of hours to resolve.

The cost in having a lawyer review a contract document,
before it is signed, is nearly always less than the cost of
having the lawyer resolve a dispute which arises subsequently, because some ambiguous provision in the contract which could have been clarified, was not fully understood by the parties when the agreement was entered into.

COMMON MISTAKE NO. 4:
Believing a Competent Lawyer Is Impossible to Find

While the competence of some lawyers can no doubt be questioned, there are many more who are competent. Finding a competent lawyer may seem difficult, but it is by no means impossible or more expensive. Remember that no lawyer is competent in all fields of the law. Therefore, it is important to ascertain the experience of the lawyer under consideration in the field of law to which your legal need relates. The mere fact that a lawyer claims to be competent in a particular field of law is not sufficient. You must make your own investigation, including asking the questions suggested in Chapter Three, to determine if the lawyer under consideration for employment is, in fact, competent.

COMMON MISTAKE NO. 5:
Waiting for a Legal Problem to Develop

Even when a legal problem is recognized, some people consider it safe to wait until the problem becomes serious before contacting a lawyer. What these people do not know is that in nearly every instance, such waiting results in more legal fees being paid to the lawyer, once he is finally consulted. Most legal problems can be responded to promptly and quickly by a lawyer trained to provide the needed service, and will be done so at a minimal cost. But once the problem becomes more serious, the cost of solving the problem is substantially greater.

"When trouble is sensed well in advance, it can easily be remedied; if you wait for it to show itself, any medicine will be too late because the disease will have become incurable."

Niccolo Machiavelli

COMMON MISTAKE NO. 6:
Relying on the Advice of a Lawyer
Representing the Other Party
to a Transaction

For some, the desire to avoid hiring a lawyer and incurring legal fees motivates them to seek "free" advice from a lawyer representing someone else. On the surface, this may seem an excellent way to avoid legal fees. But what one forgets is that the lawyer was hired to give advice to the other person, not one's self. Unless the lawyer violates his professional responsibility, in which case his advice is likely to be of little value, the person who hired the lawyer originally is the only one who will benefit from such advice, and any "free" advice received on the side is, at best, questionable.

**THE BEST TIME
TO CONSULT A LAWYER**

The very best way to use a lawyer is to get his advice on
how to avoid a legal problem. Of course, this presupposes
that you consult with him before the problem arises. If you
do not, a lawyer's advice is almost always limited to how a
problem can be contained and what action can be taken to
resolve it.

The proportionate amount of time lawyers spend on problem avoidance versus problem-solving is unknown. But it is
safe to say that most lawyers spend a substantially greater
part of their time in solving rather than preventing legal
problems. Some lawyers, and many clients, have difficulty
in detecting a potential legal problem in time to take the
right steps to prevent it, avoid it if the problem does arise, or
at least try to minimize its adverse impact on the client.
Such detection requires substantial effort, and is only developed through experience and by considerable mental
effort. The more experienced lawyers, who have dealt with
numerous client problems over the years, and have learned
in the process of solving legal problems how they arose, are
generally best able to detect a potential legal problem.
Clients who have become sophisticated in the use of lawyers, and in their ability to consult with a lawyer in time to
avoid a potential legal problem, almost always developed
such abilities by experience.

There are no hard and fast rules to help the inexperienced
to detect a potential legal problem. About all that can be
said in this regard is that you should carefully consider the
need to consult with a lawyer whenever: (1) an oral or
written contract is to be entered into, in which a personal or
monetary obligation is to be incurred; (2) you have a claim

to assert; (3) you must respond to a claim asserted by
someone else; (4) you have sustained a personal injury; (5)
you are unable to meet your obligations; or (6) you wish to
plan for the future in terms of personal development, business growth, or estate planning.

PRACTICING PREVENTIVE LAW:
THE BEST PROTECTION

Few would argue with the observation that it costs less to
prevent a problem than it does to cure that problem. When
the problem is a legal one, there are not only direct costs
involved in solving the problem, such as legal fees, but also
indirect costs including one's time and personal stress. As
the cost of legal services continue to grow at alarming rates,
it is becoming apparent that more and more people are
turning to preventive law as the way of dealing with legal
problems. Indeed, it may be the best, and perhaps only,
way of effectively controlling the cost of legal services.

The observation that with legal problems the cost of prevention is less than the cost of cure was probably first made
by large companies. Because of the very nature of their
operations, many large companies experience a continual
need for legal services. Faced with ever-increasing legal
fees, feelings of being abused by the excesses of lawyers in
charging $100 or more per hour for legal services never
justified, and promised results never obtained, and doubts
as to the efforts of many lawyers to concern themselves
with legal problem prevention, which would mean reduced
legal fees to those lawyers, many companies began hiring
lawyers as employees rather than in the traditional manner
of selecting a lawyer from private practice as the need for
specific services arose.

By doing so, it was believed that more control could be exercised over what the lawyer actually did and what his services would cost. Significantly, some of these companies have seen legal fee costs drop from $100 per hour or more for a private practice lawyer to $40 per hour or less for a so-called "in house" or company lawyer. In addition to direct savings in the form of reduced legal service costs, many of these companies found that company lawyers tended to be more concerned with and successful at preventing legal problems from developing.

Now, it is common for successful companies to employ preventive law techniques, such as using company lawyers to respond to consumer demands, product safety issues, shareholder inquiries, unfair competition claims, and various governmental regulatory agency activities. All of this is done for the purpose of preventing legal problems from reaching the costly state of litigation, and is based on hard lessons of the past which demonstrate that the cost of preventing a legal problem is less than the cost of curing it.

You can use the same techniques to avoid legal problems and their resulting costs. At the very least, such techniques can assist you in detecting a legal problem early, at a time when prompt action will minimize the cost of solving that problem. Obviously, few of us desire or are in a financial position where we can hire a lawyer to follow us around and advise us on the legal consequences of our various intended actions. But we can, and should, utilize the warning signs which tend to become obvious when we take the time to periodically review the state of our personal, family, and business affairs. To assist in this regard, a legal checkup list is enclosed as Appendix A and is intended as your guide for such a periodic review. The benefits of such a review can be stated as follows:

BENEFITS OF LEGAL CHECKUP REVIEW

Timely Discovery of
Legal Needs

By periodically reviewing a legal checkup list containing reference to those matters frequently giving rise to legal needs or problems, you are more likely to discover that need or problem early, when proper attention can be given to it so you can avoid, or at least minimize, any damage or injury which might otherwise result from inattention.

Proper Evaluation of
Legal Risks

The early discovery of a legal need or problem will make it possible for a lawyer to evaluate your need or problem in the light of available alternatives, and advise you of the risk factor involved in selecting among the various alternatives. You are then in a position to make an informed decision on what action you wish to take in response to your need or problem.

Advice to Avoid
Legal Problems

For many lawyers, one of the most frustrating aspects of practicing law involves representing clients who, aware of a legal need or problem, fail to take action to respond to that need or problem at a time when resulting damage to the client could have been avoided or at least greatly minimized. In many instances, a few minutes of a lawyer's time, at a minimal cost, would have resulted in the client receiving timely advice on how to respond to a known legal need or problem, and thus permitted the client to avoid years of involvement in a costly and time-consuming lawsuit.

Reduce Cost for
Legal Services

By now it should be obvious that the primary benefit of a periodic legal checkup review is to give you early notice of your legal needs or problems, permit you and your lawyer to properly evaluate the legal risks involved, assist you in obtaining the advice required to avoid or respond to that need or problem, and thereby greatly reduce the cost of necessary legal services.

A Concluding Comment

If, as is claimed, a major function of the organized legal profession is public service, then the legal profession could greatly improve its public image by developing an increased awareness among members of the public to the benefits to be derived from the effective practice of preventive law as a means of preventing legal problems. Such public service could take many forms, including educational seminars on preventive law conducted by lawyers in the community, the use of all forms of the media to inform members of the public on how to maintain good "legal health," and training in preventive law in the form of educational courses so that all students and not just those enrolled in law school could learn how to avoid or minimize legal problems. The benefits from such efforts are obvious.

Legal Checkup List

Since it would be impractical, if not impossible, to include in a single list every possible item which might indicate a legal need, the following checkup list is offered merely as a guide to assist you in discovering, in a timely fashion, your legal service needs.

Is such a list important? The answer, as might be expected from a lawyer, is both yes and no. In and of itself, the list has little or no benefit. But if you use the list periodically (a *minimum* of twice a year is suggested), it can prove invaluable.

Why should you use such a list? Practicing preventive law and timely discovery of legal service needs are your primary weapons against legal problems and legal fees. A few minutes spent twice a year (or more frequently) in reviewing such a list can save you days, months, or even years of worry and concern as well as time in coping with legal problems allowed to go unattended at a point when needed legal services could have been applied quickly and effectively, at a minimal cost.

How should you use this list? Read through the entire list to determine what writings, records, and documents you will need to accumulate in order to respond to each of the

various items applicable to you. Then, after accumulating
these materials, carefully review each item and ask yourself
the following questions as you do so:

- Do I have the information needed to respond fully?
- What additional information do I need?
- Where can I obtain such information?
- How can the information be obtained?
- When did I conduct my last review?
- Since my last review, has anything occurred to change
my position as it relates to this matter?
- Am I fully aware of the ramifications of such a change?
- Do I need the assistance of a lawyer or other professional
advisor?
- When should I conduct my next review?
- Have I noted on my calendar a specific date for my next
review?

You will probably think of additional questions to ask yourself as you review the various items contained in the following list. Your particular circumstances may necessitate your
adding to the following list those items which are uniquely
related to your personal, family, or business matters. And as
you go through the list, be sure you have a pen or pencil
and paper so you can write down your responses.

What should I do after completing my review? If a legal
service need is indicated, take the necessary steps, as
suggested in this book, to obtain that assistance. Also, keep
one copy of your responses with your personal papers and,
if married, give your spouse a copy. Consider giving an
additional copy to your lawyer or other professional advisor
for easy reference in the event of an emergency. Finally, do
not forget to reserve a date in the future, no more than six

months hence, for another "legal checkup" review. You can do this simply by making a notation on your home or office calendar page reflecting the date on which you will next conduct a review.

PERSONAL DATA

Name:_____

Permanent Address:_____

_____

_____

Date of last legal checkup:_____

Date of next legal checkup: _____

Calendared: _____yes _____no

Name and address of lawyer: _____

_____

_____

_____

Name and address of accountant:_____

_____

_____

_____

Appendix A

Name and address of insurance agent(s): _____

_____

_____

_____

Date and place of birth: _____

_____

Birth Certificate: ____yes ____no

Location:_____

Social Security Number:_____

United States Citizen: ____yes ____no

Naturalized: ____yes ____no

Naturalization Certificate Number:_____

Certificate of Citizenship Number: _____

Adopted: ____yes ____no

Date and place of adoption _____

_____

Power of Attorney Executed: ____yes ____no

Type of power: ____limited ____general

170   Name and address of grantee of power:_____

_____

_____

_____

Date of execution:_____

Expiration date of power: _____

Right of expectation from estate of others: ____yes ____no

Date last financial statement prepared: _____

By whom:_____

_____

_____

Copy of financial statement: ____yes ____no

Location:_____

Name and address of person to notify

in event of emergency: _____

_____

_____

_____

MARITAL STATUS

Name of spouse: _____

Date and place of marriage:_____

Appendix A

Date and place of birth of spouse: _____

Social Security Number of spouse: _____

Marriage Certificate: ____yes ____no

Location:_____

Prenuptial Agreement: ____yes ____no

Location:_____

List of community property prepared: ____yes ____no

Location:_____

List of separate property prepared: ____yes ____no

Location:_____

Gifts to spouse: ____yes ____no

List: _____

_____

Name of prior spouse: _____

Date and place of prior marriage: _____

Final divorce decree obtained: ____yes ____no

Spousal support agreement: ____yes ____no

Location:_____

Child support agreement: ____yes ____no

Location:_____

Property settlement agreement: ____yes ____no

Location:_____

Separation agreement: _____yes _____no

Location:_____

CHILDREN

Name:_____

Date and place of birth: _____

Birth Certificate: _____yes _____no

Location:_____

Name:_____

Date and place of birth: _____

Birth Certificate: _____yes _____no

Location:_____

Name:_____

Date and place of birth: _____

Birth Certificate: _____yes _____no

Location:_____

Adopted children: _____yes _____no

Adoption papers: _____yes _____no

Location:__ _____

OTHER FAMILY MEMBERS WHO ARE DEPENDENTS

Name: _____

Date and place of birth: _____

Relationship: _____

Description of support: _____

Name: _____

Date and place of birth: _____

Relationship: _____

Description of support: _____

EMPLOYMENT

Name and address of employer: _____

_____

_____

_____

Date employment began: _____

Salary: _____ Next increase due: _____

Employment agreement: ____yes ____no

Location: _____

Member of union: ____yes ____no

Name, address and local number of union:_____

_____

_____

Amount of dues:_____ Date(s) of payment:_____

Copy union/employer agreement: ____yes ____no

Location:_____

Employment benefits: ____Vacation ____Hospitalization

Profit-Sharing:____ Agreement: ____yes ____no

Term:_____ Pension:____yes ____no

Description of rights:_____

_____

_____

_____

_____

_____

Other: _____

Workmen's compensation benefits: ____yes ____no

Social Security benefits: ____yes ____no

REAL ESTATE

Description of real estate owned: _____

_____

_____

_____

_____

_____

_____

_____

Name(s) in which title held: _____

_____

_____

_____

_____

How title held: _____

Separate Property: _____ Community Property: _____

Joint Tenancy: _____ Tenancy in the entirety: _____

Other: _____

Description: _____

_____

_____

_____

_____

Date acquired: _____

Purchase price: _____

Current market value: _____

Name of seller: _____

_____

_____

_____

Deed recorded: ____yes ____no

Name(s) on deed: _____

_____

_____

_____

Title insurance: ____yes ____no

Title option: ____yes ____no

Policy Number:_____ Date obtained: _____

From whom:_____

Appendix A

Encumbrances: ____yes ____no

Mortgage:____ Lien:____ Deed of trust:____

Other: _____

Name of Mortgagee: _____

Balance due on encumbrance: _____

Monthly payment: _____

Date last payment due: _____

Property improvements: ____yes ____no

List of same: ____yes ____no

Appraisal report: ____yes ____no Date:_____

Condition of property: _____

Date of last inspection: _____

Report of inspection: ____yes ____no

Defective conditions repaired: ____yes ____no

Existing property damage: ____yes ____no

Need for improvements: ____yes ____no

Assessments: ____yes ____no

Description: _____

_____

_____

_____

Zoning classification: _____

Real Property Tax payment due: _____

Amount: _____

Deed restrictions: ____yes ____no

Description: _____

_____

_____

_____

_____

Description of all leases:

Landlord:____ Tenant:____

Term: _____

Expiration date: _____

Option to renew: ____yes ____no

Expiration date of option to renew:_____

Monthly rental: _____

Copy of each lease: ____yes ____no

Location:_____

Amendments to lease: ____yes ____no

Location:_____

Appendix A

Landlord:_____ Tenant:_____

Term:_____

Expiration date: _____

Option to renew: _____yes _____no

Expiration date of option to renew:_____

Monthly rental: _____

Copy of each lease: _____yes _____no

Location:_____

Amendments to lease: _____yes _____no

Location:_____

Landlord:_____ Tenant:_____

Term:_____

Expiration date: _____

Option to renew: _____yes _____no

Expiration date of option to renew:_____

Monthly rental: _____

Copy of each lease: _____yes _____no

Location:_____

Amendments to lease: _____yes _____no

Location:_____

PERSONAL PROPERTY

List of all valuable property: ____yes ____no

Location:_____

Current value assigned: ____yes ____no Date: _____

Record of purchase: ____yes ____no

Location:_____

Amount of lien or monthly payment due: _____

Photographs of valuable property: ____yes ____no

Location:_____

Property marked for identification: ____yes ____no

Nature of mark: _____

Insurance against loss or damage: ____yes ____no

Record of insurance: ____yes ____no

Location:_____

Description of insurance: _____

_____

_____

_____

_____

AUTOMOBILE(S)

Make: _____

Model: _____

Year: _____

Serial Number: _____

Name and address of title owner: _____

_____

_____

_____

Name and address of co-owner, if any: _____

_____

_____

_____

Name and address of finance company: _____

_____

_____

_____

Monthly payment:_____ Balance due: _____

Automobile insurance: ____yes ____no

Bodily injury: ____yes ____no Limits: _____

Expiration date: _____

Property damage: ____yes ____no Limits:_____

Expiration date: _____

Public liability: ____yes ____no Limits: _____

Expiration date: _____

Uninsured motorists: ____yes ____no Limits: _____

Expiration date: _____

Other (specify):_____ Limits: _____

Expiration date: _____

INSURANCE
Type of Policy:
Automobile:

____yes ____no Policy number: _____

Name and address of insurer: _____

_____

_____

_____

Date policy purchased:_____

Next payment due: _____

Description of coverage: _____   183

Bodily injury liability: ____yes ____no

Amount each person: _____

Amount each occurrence: _____

Medical payments: ____yes ____no Amount: _____

Property damage: ____yes ____no Amount: _____

Comprehensive liability coverage: ____yes ____no

Amount: _____

Collision: ____yes ____no Amount: _____

Deductible: ____yes ____no Amount: _____

Exclusions: _____

Procedure for filing claim: _____

Time limit:_____ Where:_____

Date of last review for adequacy of coverage:_____

Name and address of agent:_____

_____

_____

_____

184   **Accident and Health Insurance:**

_____yes _____no Policy number: _____

Name and address of insurer: _____

_____

_____

_____

Date policy purchased:_____

Next payment due: _____

Description of benefits:_____

_____

_____

_____

_____

Exclusions: _____

_____

_____

Procedure for filing claim: _____

_____

Date of last review for adequacy of coverage:_____

Name and address of agent:_____

_____

_____

_____

Life:

____yes ____no Policy number: _____

Beneficiary designation: _____

Name and address of owner:_____

_____

_____

_____

Name and address of insurer: _____

_____

_____

_____

Type of policy: _____

Date policy purchased:_____

Next payment(s) due: _____

186

Description of benefits: _____

_____

_____

_____

_____

Exclusions: _____

_____

_____

Procedure for filing claim: _____

Date of last review for adequacy of coverage:_____

Date of last review concerning beneficiary designation: __

Name and address of agent:_____

_____

_____

_____

Property Damage:

____yes ____no Policy number: _____

Name and address of insurer: _____

_____

_____

_____

Date policy purchased:_____

Next payment(s) due: _____

Description of coverage: _____

Exclusions: _____

Procedure for filing claim: _____

Time limit:_____ Where:_____

Date of last review for adequacy of coverage:_____

Name and address of agent:_____

_____

_____

_____

Fire:

____yes ____no Policy number: _____

Name and address of insurer: _____

_____

_____

_____

Date policy purchased:_____

Next payment(s) due: _____

Description of coverage: _____

_____

_____

_____

_____

Exclusions: _____

_____

_____

Procedure for filing claim: _____

Time limit:_____ Where:_____

Date of last review for adequacy of coverage:_____

Name and address of agent:_____

_____

_____

_____

Public Liability:

____yes ____no Policy number: _____

Name and address of insurer: _____

_____

_____

_____

Date policy purchased:_____

Next payment(s) due: _____

Description of coverage: _____

_____

_____

_____

_____

Exclusions: _____

_____

_____

_____

Procedure for filing claim: _____

Time limit:_____ Where:_____

Date of last review for adequacy of coverage:_____

Name and address of agent:_____

_____

_____

_____

Other:

Specify:_____

_____

_____

TAXES

Federal income taxes paid: ____yes ____no

Date:_____

Copy of tax return retained: ____yes ____no

Location:_____

State income taxes paid: ____yes ____no

Date:_____

Copy of tax return retained: ____yes ____no

Location:_____

Real estate taxes paid: ____yes ____no

Date:_____

Copy of tax return retained: ____yes ____no

Location:_____

Personal property taxes paid: ____yes ____no

Date:_____

Copy of tax return retained: ____yes ____no

Location:_____

Gift taxes paid: ____yes ____no

Date:_____

Copy of tax return retained: ____yes ____no

Location:_____

FICA taxes on household employees paid:

_____yes _____no

Date: _____

Copy of tax return retained: _____yes _____no

Location:_____

Other taxes paid (specify): _____yes _____no

Date: _____

Copy of tax return retained: _____yes _____no

Location:_____

Copy of tax returns for last five years: _____yes _____no

Location:_____

CONTRACTUAL RIGHTS

Subject matter of contract(s): _____

_____

_____

Date of contract(s): _____

Written contract: _____yes _____no

Description of contractual right: _____

_____

_____

_____

Date benefit to be received:_____

Contract rights secured: ____yes ____no

Nature of security:_____

_____

_____

CONTRACTUAL OBLIGATIONS

Name and address of individual/entity
to whom made: _____

_____

_____

_____

Description of obligation:_____

_____

_____

_____

_____

Amount of obligation:_____

Written record of obligation: ____yes ____no

Location:_____

Date and manner in which obligation to be paid: _____

_____

_____

Obligation secured: ____yes ____no

Nature of security:_____

Claim of offset: ____yes ____no

Describe: _____

INVESTMENTS

Name and address of person/entity
with whom made:_____

_____

_____

_____

Date made:_____

Written record of investment: ____yes ____no

Location:_____

Return on investment as represented: ____yes ____no

Periodic reports on investment received: ____yes ____no

In writing: ____yes ____no Date of last report:_____

Last date investment reviewed: _____

194 **STOCKS, BONDS, MUTUAL FUNDS,
AND OTHER SECURITIES**

Name and address of companying issuing: ＿＿＿＿＿＿

＿＿＿＿＿＿＿＿＿＿＿＿＿＿＿＿＿＿＿＿＿＿

＿＿＿＿＿＿＿＿＿＿＿＿＿＿＿＿＿＿＿＿＿＿

＿＿＿＿＿＿＿＿＿＿＿＿＿＿＿＿＿＿＿＿＿＿

Nature or type of security: ＿＿＿＿＿＿＿＿＿

＿＿＿＿＿＿＿＿＿＿＿＿＿＿＿＿＿＿＿＿＿＿

Name in which security held: ＿＿＿＿＿＿＿＿

Name and address of co-owner, if any: ＿＿＿＿

＿＿＿＿＿＿＿＿＿＿＿＿＿＿＿＿＿＿＿＿＿＿

＿＿＿＿＿＿＿＿＿＿＿＿＿＿＿＿＿＿＿＿＿＿

＿＿＿＿＿＿＿＿＿＿＿＿＿＿＿＿＿＿＿＿＿＿

Date of purchase: ＿＿＿＿＿＿＿＿＿＿＿＿＿

Proof of ownership: ＿＿yes ＿＿no

Original value:＿＿＿＿ Present value: ＿＿＿＿

Annual income:＿＿＿＿ Maturity date:＿＿＿＿

Name and address of agent or broker: ＿＿＿＿

＿＿＿＿＿＿＿＿＿＿＿＿＿＿＿＿＿＿＿＿＿＿

＿＿＿＿＿＿＿＿＿＿＿＿＿＿＿＿＿＿＿＿＿＿

＿＿＿＿＿＿＿＿＿＿＿＿＿＿＿＿＿＿＿＿＿＿

BANKS AND SAVINGS INSTITUTIONS

Name and address of each depository: _____

_____

_____

_____

_____

_____

_____

_____

_____

Account Number: _____

Nature of account: _____

Separate account: ____yes ____no

Joint account: ____yes ____no

Name and address on account card: _____

_____

Interest earning rate: _____

Time deposit withdrawal date: _____

Record of deposits and withdrawals: ____yes ____no

Location:_____

CREDIT CARDS

Name and address of issuing company:_____

_____

_____

_____

Copy of agreement for issuance: ____yes ____no

Location:_____

Card number:_____

Name on card:_____

Name and address of person(s) authorized to use: _____

_____

_____

_____

Amount of monthly payments: _____

Date payment due: _____

Notification procedure on theft/loss: _____

_____

Copy of card applications: ____yes ____no

Location:_____

Name and address of issuing company: _____

_____

_____

_____

Copy of agreement for issuance: ____yes ____no

Location:_____

Card number:_____

Name on card:_____

Name and address of person(s) authorized to use: _____

_____

_____

_____

Amount of monthly payments: _____

Date payment due: _____

Notification procedure on theft/loss: _____

_____

Copy of card applications: ____yes ____no

Location:_____

Name and address of issuing company: _____

_____

_____

_____

Copy of agreement for issuance: ____yes ____no

Location:_____

Card number:_____

Name on card:_____

Name and address of person(s) authorized to use: _____

_____

_____

_____

Amount of monthly payments: _____

Date payment due: _____

Notification procedure on theft/loss: _____

_____

Copy of card applications: ____yes ____no

Location:_____

Name and address of issuing company: _____

_____

_____

_____

Copy of agreement for issuance: ____yes ____no

Location:_____

Card number:_____

Name on card:_____

Name and address of person(s) authorized to use: _____

_____

_____

_____

Amount of monthly payments: _____

Date payment due: _____

Notification procedure on theft/loss: _____

_____

Copy of card applications: ____yes ____no

Location:_____

ESTATE AND
PROBATE MATTERS

Will made: ____yes ____no Date of will: _____

Date and place where will made: _____

_____

Name and address of executor/executrix: _____

_____

_____

_____

Name and address of alternative executor/executrix: ____

_____

_____

_____

Location of will:_____

Events which have occurred since will was made:

Acquisition of assets:_____

Adoption of child: _____

Birth of child:_____

Change in financial condition: _____

Death of family member/beneficiary: _____

Divorce: _____

Appendix A

Home ownership: _____

Incurrence of liabilities: _____

Lifetime gifts: _____

Major illness: _____

Marriage: _____

Amendment to will needed: ____yes ____no

Spouse has will: ____yes ____no

Location:_____

Spouse's will part of overall estate planning:

____yes ____no

Name and address of witnesses to will execution:

_____

_____

_____

_____

_____

_____

_____

_____

Availability of witnesses: ____yes ____no

TRUST-FUND BENEFITS

Identity of trust: _____

Name of trustee: _____

Description of trust: _____

Benefits to which entitled: _____

Date benefits become due: _____

List of trust assets: ___yes ___no

Location: _____

Total value of benefits expected from trust: _____

Right to receive reports from trustee: ___yes ___no

Date last report received from trustee: _____

SAFE-DEPOSIT BOX

Have safe-deposit box: ___yes ___no

Box number: _____

Location: _____

Number of keys: _____ Location: _____

Documents in box:

Agreements: _____

Automobile papers: _____

Bank and savings account records: _____

Birth certificate: _____

Bond certificates: _____

Contracts: _____

Death certificates: _____

Deeds: _____

Divorce decree: _____

Insurance policies: _____

Licenses: _____

List of personal property: _____

List of real property: _____

Marriage certificate: _____

Military discharge papers: _____

Social Security card: _____

Stock certificates: _____

Tax records: _____

Will: _____

Inventory of safe-deposit box contents: ____yes ____no

Location: _____

Name and address of person notified of safe-deposit box:

_____

_____

_____

204   RETIREMENT BENEFITS

Source of benefits:_____

Description of benefits:_____

Date benefits begin: _____

Method of payment: _____

Annual income from benefits: _____

Rights of survivors to income: ____yes ____no

Describe: _____

Name of eligible dependents: _____

MISCELLANEOUS / COMMENTS

_____

_____

_____

_____

_____

_____

_____

_____

Directory of State Bar Associations

There are literally hundreds of bar associations throughout the United States, existing at city, county, and state levels. The list which follows is limited solely to state bar associations. In some states, all lawyers licensed to practice law in that state must be members of the state bar association. In other states, such membership is optional.

At the state bar association level, and in states where membership is mandatory, the association operates as an administrative arm of the highest court of the state and/or the legislature in matters relating to the admission, practice, discipline, and disbarment of persons applying for or licensed to practice law in the state. In states where such membership is not mandatory, the highest court of the state or the legislature performs these tasks with or without the assistance of the association.

State bar associations perform a number of valuable services including: adoption of admission standards; training of law students; providing legal aid services; placement of new lawyers; preparation and dissemination of directories and other lawyer lists; development of lawyer referral services; maintenance of professional standards and ethics; investigation of complaints against members; recommendations for disciplinary action; legislative activities in such areas as the administration of justice, courtroom procedures, jury selection, and the enactment and amendment of laws.

206　At the local community level, such associations frequently combine social, educational, professional, and political activities. While such activities and the services provided by such associations vary, they are generally responsive to inquiries both by telephone and letter, and are available to provide useful information on lawyer members, as well as to receive and investigate complaints regarding such lawyers. The address and telephone number of the local bar association in the community where you reside can be obtained from your local telephone directory. The association will probably be listed under the name of the city or county followed by the words "Bar Association."

Alabama State Bar
P.O. Box 671
Montgomery, Alabama 36101
(205) 269-1515

Alaska Bar Association
P.O. Box 279
Anchorage, Alaska 99510
(907) 272-7469

State Bar of Arizona
234 N. Central, Suite 858
Phoenix, Arizona 85004
(602) 254-4804

Arkansas Bar Association
400 W. Markham
Little Rock, Arkansas 72201
(501) 375-4605

State Bar of California
555 Franklin Street
San Francisco, California 94102
(415) 561-8200

Colorado Bar Association
University of Denver
Law Center
200 West Fourteenth Avenue
Denver, Colorado 80204
(303) 629-6873

Connecticut Bar Association
15 Lewis Street
Hartford, Connecticut 06103
(203) 249-9141

Delaware Bar Association
1207 King Street
Wilmington, Delaware 19801
(302) 658-0847

The Bar Association of the
District of Columbia
1819 H Street, N.W.
Washington, D.C. 20006
(202) 223-1480

District of Columbia Bar
1426 H Street, N.W.
Washington, D.C. 20005
(202) 638-1500

The Florida Bar
Tallahasse, Florida 32304
(904) 222-5286

State Bar of Georgia
1510 Fulton National
Bank Building
Atlanta, Georgia 30303
(404) 522-6255

Hawaii State Bar Association
P.O. Box 26
Honolulu, Hawaii 96810
(808) 537-1868

Idaho State Bar
P.O. Box 895
Boise, Idaho 83701
(208) 342-8958

Illinois State Bar Association
Illinois Bar Center
Springfield, Illinois 62701
(217) 525-1760

Indiana State Bar Association
230 E. Ohio
Indianapolis, Indiana 46204
(317) 639-5465

208

Iowa State Bar Association
1101 Fleming Building
Des Moines, Iowa 50309
(515) 243-3179

Kansas Bar Association
1334 Topeka Avenue
P.O. Box 1037
Topeka, Kansas 66601
(913) 234-5696

Kentucky Bar Association
Frankfort, Kentucky 40601
(502) 564-3795

Louisiana State
Bar Association
225 Baronne Street, Suite 210
New Orleans, Louisiana 70112
(504) 566-1600

Maine State Bar Association
P.O. Box 788
Augusta, Maine 04330
(207) 622-7523

Maryland State
Bar Association, Inc.
905 Keyser Building
Calvert & Redwood Streets
Baltimore, Maryland 21202
(301) 685-7878

Massachusetts Bar Association
One Center Plaza
Boston, Massachusetts 02108
(617) 523-4529

State Bar of Michigan
306 Townsend Street
Lansing, Michigan 48933
(517) 372-9030

Minnesota State
Bar Association
100 Minnesota Federal Building
Minneapolis, Minnesota 55402
(712) 335-1183

Mississippi State Bar
620 N. State Street
Jackson, Mississippi 39201
(601) 948-4471

The Missouri Bar
P.O. Box 119
326 Monroe
Jefferson City, Missouri 65101
(314) 635-4128

State Bar of Montana
P.O. Box 4669
Helena, Montana 59601
(406) 442-7660

Nebraska State
Bar Association
1019 Sharp Building
Lincoln, Nebraska 68508
(402) 475-7091

State Bar of Nevada
P.O. Box 2125
Reno, Nevada 89505
(702) 323-0338

New Hampshire
Bar Association
77 Market Street
Manchester,
New Hampshire 03101
(603) 669-4869

New Jersey State
Bar Association
172 West State Street
Trenton, New Jersey 08608
(609) 394-1101

State Bar of New Mexico
New Mexico Law Center
1117 Stanford Avenue, N.E.
P.O. Box 25883
Albuquerque, New Mexico 87125
(505) 842-3901
In-State Wats: 1-800-432-6976

New York State
Bar Association
One Elk Street
Albany, New York 12207
(518) 445-1211

North Carolina Bar Foundation
1025 Wade Avenue
Raleigh, North Carolina 27605
(919) 828-0561

North Carolina State Bar
P.O. Box 25850
Raleigh, North Carolina 27611
(919) 828-4620

State Bar Association   209
of North Dakota
P.O. Box 2136
Bismarck, North Dakota 58501
(701) 255-1404

Ohio State Bar Association
33 W. 11th Avenue
Columbus, Ohio 43201
(614) 421-2121

Oklahoma Bar Association
1901 North Lincoln Boulevard
P.O. Box 53036
Oklahoma City, Oklahoma 73105
(405) 524-2365

Oregon State Bar
1776 S.W. Madison
Portland, Oregon 97205
(503) 229-5788

Pennsylvania Bar Association
P.O. Box 186
Harrisburg,
Pennsylvania 17108
(717) 238-6751

Bar Association of Puerto Rico
P.O. Box 1900
San Juan, Puerto Rico 00903
(809) 724-3358

Rhode Island Bar Association
1804 Industrial Bank Building
Providence, Rhode Island 02902
(401) 421-5740

210

South Carolina Bar Association
P.O. Box 11297
Columbia, South Carolina 29211
(803) 779-6653

State Bar of South Dakota
222 E. Capitol
Pierre, South Dakota 57501
(605) 224-7554

Tennessee Bar Association
1717 W. End Avenue, Suite 600
Nashville, Tennessee 37023
(615) 329-1601
In-State Wats: 1-800-342-8618

State Bar of Texas
P.O. Box 12487
Capitol Station
Austin, Texas 78711
(512) 475-4200

Utah State Bar
425 E. First South
Salt Lake City, Utah 84101
(801) 322-1015

Vermont Bar Association
P.O. Box 100
Montpelier, Vermont 05602
(802) 223-2020

Virginia State Bar
Suite 1622, 700 Building
700 East Main Street
Richmond, Virginia 23219
(804) 786-2061

Virginia Bar Association
P.O. Box 5206
Charlottesville,
Virginia 22903
(804) 977-1396

Washington State Bar
505 Madison
Seattle, Washington 98104
(206) 622-6054

West Virginia State Bar
E-404, State Capitol
Charleston,
West Virginia 25305
(304) 346-8414

West Virginia Bar Association
P.O. Box 346
Charleston,
West Virginia 25322
(304) 342-1474

State Bar of Wisconsin
402 West Wilson Street
Madison, Wisconsin 53703
(608) 257-3838

Wyoming State Bar
P.O. Box 3388
Cheyenne, Wyoming 82001
(307) 632-9061

Public Interest Law Firms and Organizations

The following list of public interest law firms and organizations contains only a few of the many such firms and organizations which exist throughout the United States.

Since the nature, scope, and effectiveness of the services provided by some of these firms and organizations change from time to time, as do their locations, telephone numbers, and personnel, the listing of a firm or organization here is not intended as an endorsement and should not be so construed.

Just as it is important for you to make your own independent investigation and evaluation of the lawyer you intend to hire, so too must you independently investigate and evaluate the services offered by a public interest law firm or organization. The same principles set forth in this book to assist you in conducting such an evaluation of a lawyer can guide you in evaluating organizations which provide legal services.

ALABAMA

MONTGOMERY
Southern Poverty Law Center
1001 South Hull Street 36101
(205) 264-0286

ALASKA

ANCHORAGE
Alaska Public Interest Research Group
630 W. 4th Avenue 39510
(907) 287-3661 or 272-6732

ARIZONA

PHOENIX
Arizona Center for Law in the Public Interest
P.O. Box 2783 85002
(602) 252-4904

CALIFORNIA

BERKELEY
National Housing and Economic Development Law Project
2150 Shattuck Avenue, Suite 300 94704
(415) 548-2600

National Housing Law Project
2150 Shattuck Avenue, Suite 300 94704
(415) 548-9400

BEVERLY HILLS
Beverly Hills Bar Association Law Foundation
300 South Beverly Drive, Suite 201 90212
(213) 553-6644

Center for Law in the Public Interest
10203 Santa Monica Boulevard 90212
(213) 879-5588

Appendix C

1636 West 8th Street, Suite 201 90016
(213) 833-1381

SACRAMENTO
Pacific Legal Foundation
455 Capital Mall, Suite 465 95814
(916) 444-0154

SAN FRANCISCO
American Civil Liberties Union of Northern California
814 Mission Street, Suite 301 94103
(415) 777-4545

Lawyers' Committee for Urban Affairs
625 Market Street, Suite 1208 94105
(415) 543-9444

Mexican-American Legal Defense and Educational Fund,
Inc.
12 Geary Street 94108
(415) 981-5800

NAACP Legal Defense and Educational Fund, Inc.
12 Geary Street 94108
(415) 788-8736

Public Advocates, Inc.
433 Turk Street 94102
(415) 411-8850

National Center for Youth Law
693 Mission Street, 6th Floor 94105
(415) 543-3307

SAN JOSE
Santa Clara County Bar Association Law Foundation, Inc.
210 South First Street, No. 309
P.O. Box 267 95103
(408) 293-4790

214 SANTA MONICA
National Health Law Program
2401 Main Street 90405
(213) 825-7601

COLORADO

BOULDER
Native American Rights Fund
1506 Broadway 83032
(303) 831-7559

DENVER
Mexican-American Legal Defense and Education Fund
250 W. 14th Avenue, Suite 308 80204
(303) 893-1893

Migrant Legal Action Project, Inc.
1644 Emerson Street 80213
(303) 831-7751

Mountain States Legal Foundation
1845 Sherman Street 80203
(303) 831-0244

CONNECTICUT

NEW HAVEN
Center for Advocacy Research and Planning, Inc.
33 Whitney Avenue 60511
(203) 787-5941

Connecticut Women's Educational and Legal Fund, Inc.
614 Orange Street 06511
(203) 865-0188

DISTRICT OF COLUMBIA

Aviation Consumer Action Project
1376 Connecticut Avenue, N.W. 20036
(202) 223-4498

Center for Community Change
1000 Wisconsin Avenue, N.W. 20007
(202) 338-6310

Children's Defense Fund
1520 New Hampshire Avenue, N.W. 20036
(202) 483-1470

Citizens Communication Center
1421 16th Street, N.W., Suite 404 20036
(202) 296-4238

Common Cause
2030 M Street, N.W. 20036
(202) 833-1200

Consumers Union
1714 Massachusetts Avenue, N.W. 20036
(202) 785-1906

Environmental Defense Fund, Inc.
1525 18th Street, N.W. 20036
(202) 833-1484

Food Research and Action Center
2011 Eye Street, N.W. 20006
(202) 452-8250

Institute for Public Interest Representation
Georgetown University Law Center
600 New Jersey Avenue, N.W. 20001
(202) 624-8390

Lawyers' Committee for Civil Rights Under Law
733 15th Street, N.W., Suite 427 20005
(202) 628-6700 (National Office)

Lawyers' Committee for Civil Rights Under Law
733 15th Street, N.W., Suite 520 20005
(202) 628-6700 (Washington, D.C. Committee)

Legal Research and Service for the Elderly
(National Council of Senior Citizens)
1551 K Street, N.W. 20005
(202) 638-4351

Mental Health Law Project
1220 Nineteenth Street, N.W., Suite 300 20036
(202) 467-5730

Mexican-American Legal Defense and Educational Fund
1028 Connecticut Avenue, N.W., Suite 716 20036
(202) 659-5166

Migrant Legal Action Program, Inc.
806 15th Street, N.W., Suite 600 20005
(202) 347-5100 or (800) 424-9425

National Center for Law and the Deaf
Seventh and Florida Avenues, N.W. 20002
(202) 447-0445

National Housing Law Project
1016 16th Street, N.W., Suite 800 20036
(202) 659-0050

National Prison Project of the
American Civil Liberties Union Foundation
1346 Connecticut Avenue, N.W., Suite 1031 20036
(202) 331-0500

National Resource Center for Consumers of Legal Services
1302 18th Street, N.W. 20036
(202) 659-8514

National Senior Citizen Law Center
1200 15th Street, N.W., Suite 500 20005
(202) 872-1404

Appendix C

National Social Science and Law Project
1990 M Street, N.W., Suite 610 20036
(202) 223-4315

NOW Legal Defense and Education Fund
1029 Vermont Avenue, N.W., Suite 800 20005
(202) 347-2279

Pacific Legal Foundation
1990 M Street, N.W., Suite 550 20036
(202) 466-2686

FLORIDA

MIAMI BEACH
Legal Research and Services for the Elderly
Florida Office
407 Lincoln Road 33139
(305) 534-4721

GEORGIA

ATLANTA
Southeastern Legal Foundation, Inc.
1800 Century Boulevard, N.W., Suite 950 30345
(404) 325-2255

ILLINOIS

CHICAGO
Lawyers for the Creative Arts
111 N. Wabash Avenue 60602
(312) 263-6989

Prisoners' Legal Assistance
343 S. Dearborn 60604
(312) 996-5540

INDIANA

SOUTH BEND
The National Center for Law and the Handicapped, Inc.
1235 N. Eddy Street 46617
(219) 288-4751

LOUISIANA

NEW ORLEANS
Louisiana Center for the Public Interest
700 Maison Blanche Building 70112
(504) 524-1231

MARYLAND

BALTIMORE
Developmental Disabilities Law Project
University of Maryland School of Law
500 West Baltimore Street 21201
(301) 528-6307

MASSACHUSETTS

BOSTON
National Consumer Law Center, Inc.
11 Beacon Street 02108
(617) 523-8010

CAMBRIDGE
Center for Law and Education, Inc.
Gutman Library, 3rd Floor
6 Appian Way 02138
(617) 495-4666

MICHIGAN

DETROIT
Michigan Legal Services
900 Michigan Building
220 Bagley 48226
(313) 964-4130

Appendix C

MINNEAPOLIS
Legal Rights Center, Inc.
808 E. Franklin Avenue 55404
(612) 871-4886

MISSISSIPPI

JACKSON
Lawyers' Committee for Civil Rights Under Law
720 Milner Building, 210 S. Lamar Street
P.O. Box 1971 39205
(601) 948-5400

NEW JERSEY

NEWARK
Rutgers Constitutional Litigation Clinic
Rutgers State University of New Jersey School of Law
175 University Avenue 07102
(201) 648-4687

NEW YORK

NEW YORK CITY
American Civil Liberties Union
22 East 40th Stret 10016
(212) 725-1222

Center for Constitutional Rights
853 Broadway 10003
(212) 674-3303

Center on Social Welfare Policy and Law
95 Madison Avenue 10016
(212) 679-3709

220   Employment Rights Project
Columbia Law School
435 West 116th Street 10027
(212) 280-4291

Environmental Defense Fund, Inc.
475 Park Avenue South 10016
(212) 593-2185

Handicapped Persons Legal Support Unit
335 Broadway, Room 803 10013
(212) 925-1000

Legal Action Center
271 Madison Avenue 10016
(212) 670-6502

Legal Services for the Elderly Poor
2095 Broadway, Room 304 10023
(212) 595-1340

Mental Health Law Project
84 Fifth Avenue 10011
(212) 924-7800

NAACP Legal Defense and Educational Fund, Inc.
10 Columbus Circle, Suite 2030 10019
(212) 586-8397

National Conference of Black Lawyers, Inc.
126 West 119th Street 10026
(212) 866-3501

National Emergency Civil Liberties Committee
25 East 26th Street 10010
(212) 683-8120

New York Civil Liberties Union
84 Fifth Avenue 10011
(212) 924-7800

New York Public Interest Research Group, Inc.   **221**
5 Beekman Street 10038
(212) 349-6460

Puerto Rican Legal Defense and Education Fund, Inc.
95 Madison Avenue 10016
(212) 532-8470

ROCHESTER
Greater Up-State Law Project
80 West Main Street 14614
(716) 325-2520

OHIO

COLUMBUS
Southeastern Ohio Legal Services Program
Central Office
155 North High Street, 4th Floor 43215
(614) 221-2668

OREGON

PORTLAND
Northwest Environmental Defense Center
10015 Terwilliger Boulevard 97219
(503) 244-7171, ext. 545

1000 Friends of Oregon
407 Dekum Building
519 Southwest Third Avenue 97204
(503) 233-4396

PENNSYLVANIA

PHILADELPHIA
Mid-Atlantic Legal Foundation
1521 Locust Street, Suite 600 19102
(215) 545-1913

TEXAS

SAN ANTONIO
Mexican-American Legal Defense and Education Fund
201 North St. Mary's Street 78205
(512) 224-5476

SAN JUAN
Oficina Legal del Puerto Unido
P.O. Box 1493 78589
(512) 787-8171

VIRGINIA

ARLINGTON
Tax Analysts and Advocates
2369 North Taylor Street 22207
(703) 522-1800

WISE
Concerned Citizens for Justice, Inc.
P.O. Box 1409 24293
(703) 328-9239

WASHINGTON

SEATTLE
Northwest Labor and Employment Law Office
1812 East Madison Street 98122
(206) 324-3181

WEST VIRGINIA

CHARLESTON
Appalachian Research and Defense Fund, Inc.
1116-B Kanawha Boulevard East 25301
(314) 344-9687

West Virginia Citizens Action Group
1324 Virginia Street East 25301
(304) 346-5891

Appendix C

WISCONSIN

MADISON
Center for Public Representation
520 University Avenue 53073
(608) 251-4008

Bibliography

For those readers who desire more information on the various subjects mentioned in this book, the following bibliography, representing only a sample of the many outstanding reading materials available, is offered. Contact the publisher or institution shown for information on how you can obtain a copy of these books and periodicals.

Many local and state bar associations, as well as the American Bar Association, publish and offer, either free or for a nominal fee, informational pamphlets to assist non-lawyers in dealing with lawyers and the legal system. For specific information, or merely to find out what materials are available, write or telephone your local or state bar association, or write to the American Bar Association at 1155 East 60th Street, Chicago, Illinois 60637.

Still another excellent source for information is the National Clearing House for Legal Services at 500 N. Michigan Avenue, Chicago, Illinois 60611. This non-profit corporation, funded by the Legal Services Corporation, maintains a document reprint service and makes available for a nominal fee many excellent articles on a variety of legal subjects.

Public Access to   225
Legal Services

Cheatham, Elliott Evans, *A Lawyer When Needed*. New York: Columbia University Press, 1963.

Christensen, Barlow F., *Lawyers for People of Moderate Means: Some Problems of Availability of Legal Services*. Chicago: American Bar Foundation, 1970.

Curran, Barbara A., *The Legal Needs of the Public: The Final Report of a National Survey*. Chicago: American Bar Foundation, 1977.

Handler, Joel F., Hollingsworth, Ellen Jane, and Erlanger, Howard S., *Lawyers and the Pursuit of Legal Rights*. New York: Academic Press, 1978.

Marks, F. Raymond, *The Legal Needs of the Poor: A Critical Analysis*. Chicago: American Bar Foundation, 1971.

Professional
Responsibility

Freedman, Monroe H., *Lawyers' Ethics in an Adversary System*. Indianapolis: The Bobbs-Merrill Company, Inc., 1975.

Hazard, Geoffrey C., Jr., *Ethics in the Practice of Law*. New Haven: Yale University Press, 1978.

Kaufman, Andrew L., *Problems in Professional Responsibility*. Boston: Little Brown & Company, 1976.

Marks, F. Raymond, *The Lawyer, the Public, and Professional Responsibility*. Chicago: American Bar Foundation, 1972.

Marks, F. Raymond, and Cathcart, Darlene, *Discipline Within the Legal Profession: Is it Self-Regulated?* Chicago: American Bar Foundation, 1974.

226   *Professional Responsibility: A Guide for Attorneys.* Chicago: American Bar Association Press, 1978.

Lawyer
Specialization

"Chief Justice Burger Proposes First Steps Toward Certification of Trial Advocacy Specialists." *American Bar Association Journal,* Vol. 60, February, 1974.

Franson, David, "Let's Be Realistic About Specialization." *American Bar Association Journal,* Vol. 63, January, 1977.

Legal Specialization. Chicago: American Bar Association Press, 1976.

"Specialization: Special Skills of Advocacy." *Florida Bar Journal,* Vol. 48, No. 3, March, 1974.

Legal
Fees

MacKinnon, F. B., *Contingent Fees for Legal Services: A Study of Professional Economics and Responsibilities.* Chicago: Aldine Publishing Company, 1964.

Legal Service
Plans

Deitch, Lillian, and Weinstein, David, *Prepaid Legal Services: Socioeconomic Impacts.* Lexington, Ky.: Lexington Books, 1976.

Hayes, Stephen M., and Koff, Gail J., *Legal Delivery Systems: Available Alternatives.* New York: Practising Law Institute, 1977.

Marks, F. Raymond, Hallauer, Robert Paul, and Clifton, Richard R., *The Shreveport Plan: An Experiment in the Delivery of Legal Services.* Chicago: American Bar Foundation, 1974.

Bibliography

Public Interest Law

Ashman, Allan, "The New Private Practice." Washington, D. C.: National Legal Aid and Defender Association, 1972.

Berlin, Edward, Roisman, Anthony, and Kessler, Gladys, "Public Interest Law." Washington, D. C.: *George Washington Law Review,* Vol. 28, No. 4, May, 1970.

Ehrlich, Thomas, "A Progress Report from the Legal Services Corporation." Chicago: *American Bar Association Journal,* Vol. 62, September, 1976.

Halpern, Charles R., and Cunningham, John M., "Reflections on the New Public Interest Law: Theory and Practice at the Center for Law of Social Policy." Washington, D. C.: *Georgetown Law Journal,* Vol. 59, No. 5, May, 1971.

Handler, Joel F., Hollingsworth, Ellen Jane, Erlanger, Howard E., and Landinsky, Jack, "Public Interest Activities of Private Practice Lawyers." Chicago: *American Bar Association Journal,* Vol. 61, November, 1975.

Marks, F. Raymond, *The Lawyer, the Public, and Professional Responsibility.* Chicago: American Bar Foundation, 1972.

Segal, Bernard G., "The Tasks of Law in a Troubled Time." Chicago: *American Bar Association Journal,* Vol. 56, September, 1970.

"Standing: Who Speaks for the Environment?" *Montana Law Review,* Winter, 1971.

"The New Public Interest Lawyers." *The Yale Law Journal,* Vol. 79, No. 6, May, 1970.

Weisbrod, Burton A., Handler, Joel F., and Komesar, Neil K., *Public Interest Law.* Berkeley: University of California Press, 1978.

228

Preventive Law

Brown, Lewis M., *Preventive Law*. New York: Prentice-Hall, Inc., 1950.

General Reading

Auerback, Jerald S., *Unequal Justice*. New York: Oxford University Press, 1976.

Bloom, Murray Theigh, *The Trouble with Lawyers*. New York: Simon and Schuster, 1968.

Green, Mark J., *The Other Government: The Unseen Power of Washington Lawyers*. New York: W. W. Norton and Company, 1978.

Lieberman, Jethro K., *Crisis at the Bar*. New York: W. W. Norton and Company, 1978.

Nader, Ralph, and Green, Mark J., *Verdicts on Lawyers*. New York: Thomas Y. Crowell Company, 1976.

Rosenthal, Douglas E., *Lawyer and Client: Who's in Charge?* New York: Russell Sage Foundation, 1974.

Wasserstein, Bruce, and Green, Mark J., *With Justice for Some*. Boston: Beacon Press, 1972.

Index

Index

Book design and photo/Michael Patrick Cronan